MEMOIRS OF A MANSION

MEMOIRS OF A MANSION

PHYLLIS PRITCHETT DE MARTINI

Ametsa

Memoir of a Mansion -- 1st ed. in paperback
ISBN 978-2-9701510-1-2
Also available in Hardcover
First Printing, 2021

Dedicated to Frédéric

PART ONE of this book is based on newspaper articles published in the Journal d'Estavayer and Journal de la Broye from 1910 to 1980. The subjects treated and opinions expressed are those of the journalists who reported the events at the time. After photographing articles related to the neighborhood around the railway station and others I found of interest, I translated them into English. My sincere thanks go to the personnel of Media f, former Imprimerie Butty, who graciously tolerated my presence in their archives over a two-year period.

My thanks also to the many people who provided me with information and assistance. In particular; my editor, Clare O'Dea (author of The Naked Swiss and Voting Day), Richard Harvell at Bergli books whose early encouragement motivated me to continue this unconventional project, Rosmarie Binz for her tireless proofreading and unfailing support, Hervé Galeuchet for his oversight of local history and framework of the story, Jean-Pierre Grossrieder and Francis de Vevey for sharing their photo collections, Marie-France Corminboeuf for her cover painting, my neighbors Marguerite Bovet and Denis Chanez for sharing the history and lore of the neighborhood, Alain Liardet and my readers, Lorrie, Thom, and Cricket.

We go back a long way. I met her when her husband fell in love with me. Needless to say, we didn't hit it off too well in the beginning. My tall, stylish silhouette tends to attract men, architects in particular. But... I must be completely honest with you and tell you that I am not a person. I am a building. A neoclassic villa!

She was my second owner. Over the years, as she got to know me better, we became close friends. By the time I met her, I had already been through two wars and three generations of the family who built me. I had known the joy of new babies born within my walls, and together with her, sorrow over the loss of ones we loved dearly. She learned to interpret my moods and my tastes and choose furnishings that complimented my classic style. We developed a certain intimacy that facilitated communication between us, despite the obvious obstacles.

My lifetime has now spanned more than a century and I thought it would be nice to find a way to tell the story of my life and the events that happened around me. People publish their memoirs all the time, but how could I do it without a mouth to speak and a hand to write. For such a project, I needed a spokesman or rather a spokeswoman, and it had to be my owner. She was sitting on the Chinese rug in the living room looking at old Illustration magazines and cutting out advertisements from 1915. Usually, she perceives my thoughts, although I must say, sometimes she is a little slow at it.

A light breeze was coming through the window and I took advantage of it to assemble all my force and propel the idea her way.

"Write my memoirs! Write my memoirs!"

Suddenly, she looked up with a luminous expression on her face and said,

"You know, I have a great idea. I'll write your memoirs. There are a lot of new people in town who don't know what happened here during the last century. I could only tell part of it, but you could tell it all. You could be the narrator. It's a wonderful idea, don't you think?"

Ouf! That was exhausting, but she got it.

Here's my story...

PART ONE

~ 1 ~

November 1910

Although it may shock you, I was conceived on a drafting board.

It happened on a rainy day in the office of my architect, Monsieur Ernest Devolz, in the city of Fribourg. Outside the office window, rivulets of water snaked their way slowly down the glass pane while Monsieur Devolz meticulously verified every detail of the final building plan. When he was satisfied, he picked up his fountain pen, signed the plan with a flourish and I came into existence. The section at the bottom corner of the large blueprint spread across the drafting table, provided me with important information: **Ernest Devolz, Architect, Villa St-Pierre, Estavayer, Switzerland. 18 November 1910.**

Once the formalities of obtaining a building permit and registering me at the title office were completed, I could consider myself as having officially come into the world. Monsieur Devolz was a well-known architect and I was flattered that he had undertaken my construction.

It was on a chilly morning in the spring of 1911 that my physical structure came into being. The sun emerged over the Alps and dissipated the mist clinging to the surface of Lake Neuchâtel. One of its mightier rays focused a beam of light on a meadow outside the ramparts of a small medieval city. It was there that the ground would be broken for my foundation. One of my earliest memories is of Monsieur Devolz wandering around my plot of land, tapping my rolled-up building plan in the palm of his hand. He verified the reference points and markers the surveyor had staked out to establish my dimensions. He smiled at his foreman and nodded. The first shovel sliced through the grass and extracted a heavy clump of earth. My construction had begun and would continue for two more years until I stood fully erect, a proud and imposing mansion.

In the beginning, men with wheelbarrows and shovels were digging and piling up earth. Horses and wagons carried it away. The foreman shouted orders over the creaking of wagons and the slap of leather. The horses whinnied and stomped their feet. The wild rabbits, who had dug holes all over the undisturbed land, were in for a surprise. I wondered what they thought of the crater being dug for my foundation. On the edge of the excavation, a stack of granite blocks waited to be used for the base of my structure. They looked solid and durable and would carry me well into old age.

My slab was poured with waves of cool refreshing concrete. The masons leveled it out with long wooden boards they wiggled back and forth. It tickled a little as they moved the boards forward. Subtle green sandstone blocks formed the corners of my structure, which I thought looked very chic with the white masonry of my façade. Monsieur Devolz used the same green sandstone for the columns holding up my portico. He referred to my style as neo-classic. From the beginning, I thought it was quite smart looking and a bit Italian. I have a feminine appreciation for details like that. *La maison* (house) in our French language is a feminine noun. Many of my workers came from Italy. I didn't know what or where that was back then, but I noticed the way they spoke wasn't the same as that of my architect and his foreman. In those days, the first thing I heard every morning was "Buongiorno, Buongiorno," The workers shouted at each other all day, "Giuseppe, dammi una mano, presto!" (give me a hand, quick!) or "Matteo, mettilo quà." (put it there).

While my foundation was being laid, a strange bird glided overhead. The workers stopped to look up at the sky. Matteo shouted,

"It's René Grandjean, the aviation pioneer. He's going to fly across Lake Neuchâtel."

The next day, he told the others that Grandjean had developed engine trouble and barely made it back. Helped by a stiff Joran wind, he crashed into the reeds on the shoreline. It didn't look like there was going to be much of a future for airplanes.

As my construction progressed, I was becoming more aware of my surroundings. There were two hotels in the neighborhood at the time; the Bellevue and the Hotel du Lac. I was located on Avenue de la Gare between the two of them. The railway station across the street had been there since 1877. It was a fascinating place. The clop clop of the horses' hooves echoed in the damp morning air as they made their way down Avenue de la Gare to the station with their wagonloads of sugar beets. The whistle of the steam train split the air as the engine approached the station and slowed to a hissing stop, obscured in a billowing cloud of steam. Farmers shouted and maneuvered their horses, juggling for the most advantageous position on the loading dock. While the horses pawed impatiently on the ground, the sugar beets were loaded into wagons destined for the factory in Aarberg where sugar was processed and served with absinthe distilled in the Val de Travers. When the wind was from the west, it carried the smell of sweat from the horses. Station employees shoveled up the manure on the platform after the horses left. The wind carried that smell too.

The railway station and the Hotel Bellevue. You can see my rooftop between them.
Photo curtesy of Jean-Pierre Grossriede

In those days, Avenue de la Gare was lined with mothers holding their children by the hand and men in boaters leaning against their horse-drawn wagons watching my progress and exchanging rumors about who my occupants would be when the construction was finished. Every day, a stream of men and women, school children, nannies pushing prams, horses, dogs, bicycles, wagons, and Catholic nuns paraded in front of my gate on Avenue de la Gare.

The Hotel du Lac had recently been transformed and housed the Institute Stavia, a prestigious boarding school for boys. The Bellevue was an audacious, towering Art Nouveau creation.

A poster at its entrance boasted of its modern amenities; central heating, electricity, a dark room for photography, and a garage for motorcars. It had a lovely garden where ladies with sun umbrellas sat chatting and drinking tea. I liked to listen to people gossiping in front of my gate, and I learned that the guests at the Hotel Bellevue came from Paris by train. I didn't know where Paris was, but I loved to watch the ladies passing my gate in their fashionable dresses with narrow waists and puffy sleeves, topped off with elaborate wide-brimmed hats. They were accompanied by elegant gentlemen who, even though they were young and fit, carried canes.

From my portico, I could admire this *beau monde* as they strolled along the avenue. Once in a while, a gasoline-powered automobile passed by. It attracted a great deal of attention but left behind a strange exhaust smell I hadn't encountered before.

My architect and his foreman stopped their work to watch the passing of a Martini motorcar. Monsieur Devolz pointed and said,

"See that automobile! It's one of the gasoline-powered

ones. They're made in St. Blaise on the other end of the lake. They're faster than electric cars."

"But they make a lot of noise and smoke," argued the foreman. "I don't think they'll catch on."

I thought the horses were wonderful; slick and shiny with rounded rumps and long manes. Why did they want to replace these beautiful creatures with noisy, lifeless metal contraptions?

Soon, I was two floors tall and couldn't help but wonder what height I would be when I was fully built. I overheard my workers talking about twenty-story skyscrapers they had worked on in large cities. I didn't understand what they meant, but it sounded dreadful. I regretted I hadn't paid more attention to the building plans when they were available, but I felt sure Monsieur Devolz had foreseen a reasonable height for me. My foreman spoke of the frightening diseases buildings can catch; dry rot, saltpeter, mold, radon, and mildew. I hoped my owners would protect me from these disorders.

While I was contemplating my future wellbeing, the sky suddenly turned orange and I learned of another danger to my existence. Fire! The prestigious Sacred Heart Institute in our neighborhood had caught on fire. As it turned out, the students living at the institute were evacuated and thanks to the intervention of the fire department and people in the area, some of the furnishings were saved.

When my walls reached the upper floors and the rafters were attached, there was a lot of sawing and hammering. There were times when long sharp nails were pounded into my rafters and screws were turned mercilessly into my framework. It was very unpleasant, but I knew it was for my own good and necessary to build a strong and lasting structure. During these stressful periods, I distracted myself by watching the horses and carriages on Avenue de la Gare rumbling to and from the train station.

I loved the train station. It was like a miniature world. Polite people waited patiently to board the train and helped elderly passengers, while rude ones pushed and elbowed their way through the crowd. I witnessed tearful goodbyes and joyful reunions. A moment before the departure of the train, there were silent dialogues mimed through hermetic windows, neither of the participants hearing a single word. The whistle of the train as it came toward the station, told me what time it was. When the wind came from the southeast, it carried the announcements of the conductor.

You are arriving in Estavayer. This train continues on to Cheyres, Yvonand, Yverdon-les-Bains.

Next stop Cheyres.

The sun setting over the Jura turned the billowing clouds of steam pink as the train came to a screeching halt in front of the station. On Sunday evenings, the doors were barely open when a troop of schoolboys in knickerbocker suits and knee socks tumbled out of the train cars. The boys were returning to the Institute Stavia after spending the weekend at home with their families. I loved to see them pushing each other around and hear them shouting and laughing. I wondered if I would have children of my own when I was fully built. Sometimes, a group of Catholic nuns, dressed in black tunics and impeccable white wimples, stopped for a moment at the gate to admire me.

I wondered if I was Catholic too. Having been built in the State of Fribourg, a Catholic state, I supposed I was.

What a grand day it was when my roof was finished and the terracotta tiles were put in place. For a building, it's a solemn moment. It brings the individual components together to form a single unit; a new identity in the architectural world. The event was celebrated by my workers, who placed a small tree on my roof and joined Monsieur Devolz for drinks and a buffet lunch. The last thing to be installed on my roof was a tall rod with a cable that went all the way to the ground. That puzzled me at first, but I learned later, it was a lightning rod to protect me from electric currents in the clouds. The termination of my sturdy weatherproof roof arrived not a moment too soon. Suddenly, I was covered with a cold white substance that came from nowhere and settled all over me.

"Snow," the workers called it.

"It's early this year."

It was a bit worrying at first. It felt chilly on my new roof and portico. I saw that it covered not only me but also the trees, the grass, the street, and everything around me. The children shrieked with laughter as they raced down Avenue de la Gare on their wooden sleds. I discovered a new landscape where everything was white. The rabbits, who had moved their warrens to the cow pasture across the street, made crisscrossing tracks through the garden. When nighttime came, the snow sparkled in the light of the full moon. Through my float glass window panes, the moonlight cast interesting geometric patterns on my new oak floor.

The Villa St. Pierre in 1912

From the time I was old enough to take an interest in the neighborhood, I noticed a small building on the cow pasture across from me. It was on the very edge of the land close to the railroad tracks. It was the size of a storage shed, but a proper construction with an attractive traditional style. I had never seen anyone going into it, and it was too small to be inhabited. Now that winter had come, some mysterious activity was going on over there. Large blocks of ice arrived on a wagon and were moved inside and covered with straw. From the comments of the workmen passing my gate, I learned that the blocks of ice were cut from a shallow pond called the Grande Gouille, near the lake. The ice was stored in the little building, then loaded on a train car and delivered to the Cardinal brewery in Fribourg. The building was known as the Glacière Cardinal.

My land is situated just outside the ramparts of a small walled city built in the Middle Ages. From my new height, I could see over the parapets and admire the spectacular Chenaux Castle with its lofty towers and its barbican.

Chenaux Castle as I saw it from my upper floor.
Photo curtesy of Jean-Pierre Grossrieder

What an edifice! I learned later on that its construction began in 1297 and was completed by the town's historical hero, Humbert le Bâtard de Savoie before his death in 1443. That's more than 600 years. What stories the castle must have to tell. From my 2nd floor, I also have a good view of the bell tower on the collegiate church and its four watchtowers, providing surveillance in all directions. On special days, flags and banners fly from the towers of the church, and sometimes a white flag appears on the tower of the castle dungeon. I hope to learn the significance of these flags in the future.

The rooftop the farthest away from me is the convent of the Dominican nuns. While I was being built, a group of seminary students from the University of Fribourg stopped on Avenue de la Gare with their teacher. The teacher explained the history of our town and, in particular, the Dominican convent. It had functioned since 1316, also 600 years, without interruption. Having newly arrived on the architectural scene and being modest in comparison, I was humbled by these venerable structures. I didn't want to appear ungrateful to my architect, but I wouldn't have minded a few towers or a barbican. I guess they're no longer in fashion.

Closer to me and just outside the ramparts is the massive structure of the Sacred Heart Institute a boarding school for Swiss German girls, run by the Theodosian Sisters of Ingenbohl. It was built in 1905 only six years ago, so it was a lot closer to me in age. At that time, because of the terrible fire that had occurred, its roof was being rebuilt. The 180 interned students were living with local families, but classrooms were already functional. The classical façade of the Sacred Heart gives it an elegant look despite its massive volume. It's surrounded by tall trees and cheerful flower beds in the summer.

Naturally, I wanted to know why I had been built. At first, I thought I would be a school like the Stavia or a hotel like the Bellevue. But I could see I hadn't enough rooms for either of those functions. I remembered the notation on my building plan had said Villa St-Pierre. So, I must be a family villa; the most recent addition to a chic, high-class neighborhood, complete with a Casino-Theatre. I was proud to be part of this new neighborhood, the first one to be built outside the ramparts, and I felt sure that my presence would contribute to the prestige of our faubourg.

In the beginning, I didn't realize the vital part the Casino-Theatre would play in the lives of my people.

The Casino-Théâtre
Photo curtesy of Jean-Pierre Grossrieder

In 1902, le Casino-Theatre d'Estavayer had presented a production by Dr. Thurler entitled "A travers le vieux Stavayé", which was attended by 7000 persons from all over Switzerland. It was an extraordinary production that took all winter to create. The 150 actors, singers, and extras had been found among the local fishermen, craftsmen, office workers, businessmen, teachers, and children. The success of this musical production gave our neighborhood a cultural distinction that lasted for years.

The house of Jules Chanez, my closest neighbor, was built on the land beyond my backyard. The property consisted of a modest house and storage buildings for wood and construction materials. I imagined they were quite interested in my construction. I did tower over them a bit and I hope I didn't leave the impression of being pompous. It's always best to get on well with your closest neighbors.

There was also a farm building on my west side that belonged to the Bovet family. Between us is a narrow street called the Route de St-Pierre. It's a quiet street bordered by a wall on both sides. Installed in a niche in the wall is a statue of St. Pierre with the keys of the kingdom. The date 1783 is carved into its base. It's this statue that has given me the name, The Villa St-Pierre.

A flurry of activity had been going on for some time in my interior, with electricians, plumbers, painters, and decorators drilling, scraping, plastering, coating, and attaching all kinds of fixtures to my interior. I knew all this was necessary to make me not only beautiful but functional and sound. Outside, my gardens were taking shape with gravel alleys, elaborate shrubbery, and a round flower bed in front of my portico. I was delighted to see a cedar tree had been planted outside the bay window of my dining room. We would be growing up together.

When the sun slipped over the Jura and the evening air cooled my façade, an unusual sound puzzled me. It sounded like riddit-riddit. Then there would be an interval of silence and the symphony of riddit-riddit would start up again. The landscapers packing up their tools stopped to listen.

"There's a lot of wetland around Lake Neuchâtel," one of them said, "and a million frogs. I have a friend who is a fisherman on the lake. When he pushes his boat out in the evening, the frogs stop croaking and start up again as soon as he leaves the shoreline." I was grateful for that information.

A lot of progress had been made on my construction

and my exterior was nearly finished. After that, the work went on inside. The interior decorator covered my living room walls with a beautiful embroidered silk cloth. It felt luxurious against the plaster of my wall. Before installing the silk, the decorators wrote their names, G. Moser et H. Cottier, Tapissiers chez Les fils de Henri Bobaing, and the date 1912, on the plaster. Heavy green velvet drapes were installed on my windows with embroidered panels on the valences. They were held back by gold-braided passementerie.

I was delighted with the white marble fireplace that appeared in my living room and I was especially pleased with its intricately carved side panels. The latest in circulating hot water radiators were installed under my window seats, and my decorator took the trouble to cover them with an attractive gold lattice. In the arched doorways between my living room, petit salon, and dining room, there were cleverly concealed doors that slid out to divide the rooms. By the simple flick of a switch, my rooms were bathed in an aurora of light. Our country was fortunate to be one of the first in Europe to have electricity because of our numerous dams. My kitchen puzzled me. The cream-colored wooden cupboards were three meters high, which made me wonder about the height of my future occupants.

A large copper boiler with a grate at the bottom for burning coal had been installed in my basement. Two large stone basins provided a place to wash and rinse clothes. A device with two rollers squeezed the water out of the clothes before they were hung on the clotheslines. I was proud to be equipped with these modern appliances.

My ingenious architect had incorporated a smoke room in my attic. One of the chimneys on the roof was connected to the wood-burning cooking stove in the kitchen. The smoke from the stove traveled through the smoke room, where whole hams and sausages would be hung before it was evacuated through the chimney. This clever function would provide my family with delicious smoked meat on a continual basis, an advantage they would come to value in the difficult years that lay ahead of them.

No expense had been spared by my owners in choosing the elements of my interior. I must have cost them a lot of money and I wondered who they were. As far as I could see, I was finished, but still uninhabited. One night around midnight, a man coming home from a party came into my garden and urinated against the granite blocks of my foundation. Needless to say, I was appalled. Disgusted. Where were my owners? They really needed to move in now and take charge. Was I really a family villa or just a monument of some kind?

~ 2 ~

The dew was still on the grass and the bells of Prime fading into the distance when a carriage rolled up to my front steps. A dignified lady in a long black dress came through my entrance hall and looked around appreciatively. She was accompanied by her three little boys. So I was, in fact, going to have children of my own! This was the moment I had been waiting for. At last, my family had arrived and would assume responsibility for my care. I was worried at first, wondering how a woman alone with three small children could manage to care for my numerous rooms and spacious garden. It was reassuring when several more carriages and wagons arrived laden with goods and members of the household staff.

The woman was a young widow. It took me a while to get the whole story. From overhearing conversations of neighbors and friends who stopped by, I learned that the father of the family, who had made his fortune in Africa, had fallen ill and died two years before. I could imagine what a drama it must have been for this family. The youngest boy, Henry, was barely a month old at the time. I realized that I owed my existence to this valiant widow with the courage to hire an architect, take on my construction and bring me up along with her young children. If not for her, I might never have existed. For the many years we spent together, I thought of her as Madame, my patron.

Having my family arrive was a momentous event. The children skipped through the hall, excitedly explored every room, and ran up and down the stairs. They admired my ivory-colored Louis XVI sofa and chairs in the living room but were not allowed to play there. There was a lot of commotion while the baggage was unloaded and territorial disputes settled.

A gramophone, in its own polished mahogany box, sat on a table in my petit salon. It had a turntable on which the family placed 78 RPM records. A needle followed the grooves in the disk and produced music. To make that happen, a metal crank had to be turned. The sound was amplified by an elegant flower-shaped horn attached to the base. My boys loved to turn the crank. My favorite song was When Irish Eyes are Smiling. There was also Ragtime and Yankee Doodle, modern music that came from America.

The rhythm of our day was established by the bells of our Collegiate church. Matins during the night, Lauds and Prime in the morning, Sext at noon, None in the afternoon, and Vespers and Compline in the evening. Even on cloudy days and during the night, I knew what time it was. Our days unfolded against this rich tapestry of sound and would have been impoverished without it.

Until now, the limit of my observation had been my

neighborhood, the train station, and the rooftops and towers of the town. Now that my family was installed in my rooms, a new dimension opened up for me. The serious handicap of not being able to read was happily remedied by my three young children. When the two eldest came home from school, they had homework to do, consisting of mathematics, science, reading, writing, and music. By observing them every day during this homework period, I progressed rapidly in the skill of reading French, our local language. Mathematics and science were beyond my capabilities...and communication, unfortunately.

Several newspapers were delivered to the house every week and also a magazine called *Illustration* printed in Paris. I came to understand that Paris was a large group of buildings in a neighboring country called France. In this magazine, I discovered a lot of things I didn't know. There were pictures of royalty and world leaders, buildings in Paris with façades that look like mine, and an abundance of towers, arches, bridges, and statues. The advertisements in the Illustration showed clever gadgets for sharpening razor blades, silk stockings, henna to color hair, and miraculous cures for all kinds of ailments. Of course, I had to rely on my family to turn the pages. When Madame took her nap in the afternoon, the domestic help leafed through the magazines instead of doing their work. I was grateful for that. The youngest servant was often scolded for leaving newspapers lying about. She was my favorite.

I knew it was 1912 because a new calendar, the Almanach des Postes et des Télégraphes, had been hung on my kitchen wall. It had a picture of two ladies on the French Riviera in lovely billowing dresses and large-brimmed hats drinking Coca-cola. This year for the first time, schoolchildren had been granted a week's vacation at Christmas and my boys were overjoyed. They explained that the teachers needed a rest.

Jules Bersier, the driver of the postal coach, was on his way to town and stopped in to leave a parcel. He took off his derby hat with a trumpet and federal cross insignia on it when he was invited into the hall. He had left town at five o'clock that morning, as he always does, to make his rounds of the nearby towns. He said his horses got stuck in the mud in the swampy area around Avenches. Despite the long distances traveled over rutted roads, through snowdrifts in the winter, and dust in the summer, Monsieur Bersier never failed at his task. Madame said we were fortunate to have such devoted civil servants.

The Journal d'Estavayer, printed by the Imprimerie Butty, is the newspaper of our town. Madame always spread it out on the dining room table to read it, which allowed us both good visibility. With the light from the tall bay window, I could read even the smallest print. After that, the newspaper traveled around the house and was left on the table in the kitchen. A reporter had written an article about the installation of telephone lines in the district. Reunions had been called in surrounding villages. Lines between most of the villages were included in the network of our town. We also received the newspaper La Liberté, printed in Fribourg, which covered wider events. For example, the national vote on a health and accident insurance plan proposed by the Federal Government on February 4th.

The bay window in my dining room. Painting by Marie-France Corminboeuf

The cattle fair takes place in front of the castle every year. It's an important event and my boys wouldn't miss it. Everyone in the house was talking about it. Cattle buyers came from all over the area. When the transactions were completed, the cattle were shipped to their new destinations by boat or by train. It was exciting for me to watch a hundred head of cattle, pigs, and sheep going down Avenue de la Gare to the train station. Thirteen train wagons were needed to transport the cattle. There was cleaning up to do after that.

The spring of 1912 brought with it some tragic news. It was on the front page of all the newspapers and everybody in the house was talking about it. On April 15, the magnificent White Star ocean liner, Titanic, sank in the Atlantic Ocean on its maiden voyage. It was a very modern ship and considered unsinkable. Almost 1,500 unfortunate persons drowned. What a tragedy!

La Liberté published an article entitled La Catastrophe du Titanic on its front page, in which a Swiss passenger, Max Staehlin from Basel, told his chilling story.

Sunday evening, Colonel Simonius, Max Frœlicher and I, lingered after dinner, chatting until about 11 o'clock. It was a clear, starry night. The ship was advancing at full steam, and onboard everything was quiet. We said goodnight and left to go to our cabins. I was undressing when I heard a dull thud, which lasted for about ten seconds and was followed by a slight jolt of the ship. A problem never entered my mind but being of a curious nature, I went into the hallway and asked a steward what had caused the noise. He said it was nothing. I started back to my cabin but decided instead to go up on deck.

I met Colonel Simonius, and we both noticed that one of the lower decks was covered with a layer of crushed ice. At that moment, the ship let off a loud belch of steam attracting a lot of passengers to the decks. Nobody seemed alarmed. The crew was calm and when questioned said there was nothing unusual. The passengers were completely reassured when they heard the orchestra start to play. The night was still, with no wind and no fog, but bitter cold. Suddenly the ship stopped and Simonius and I saw the crew lowering lifeboats from the deck. We inquired about this and were told that it was purely a precautionary measure and there was no danger. Despite this reassurance, we went to fetch our wives and placed them near the lifeboats. It was evident that no one believed they were in imminent danger. Captain Smith, however, was nervous and ordered the lifeboats to be put to sea. At this time, we realized that the ship was in danger of sinking. I went to my cabin and took whatever valuables I had there. The music continued and despite the advice of the officers, no one wanted to go into the lifeboats. There was no panic and several ladies did not want to leave their husbands. Simonius and I went into one of the least occupied lifeboats with our wives and touched down on the water. The men of the Titanic pushed us offshore with gaffes; in each boat, men took the oars. There were 16 or 18 lifeboats, each containing 50 to 60 people. The Titanic was absolutely still in the water, the music was playing in the dining room, and none of the passengers suspected the Titanic was sinking. At one point, the ship listed to the front, and the passengers finally understood the horror of the situation. An agitated crowd began running on the deck, looking for a place in the boats. The machinists appeared in the hatches; many of them rushed to the lifeboats but were held off by the crew. The Titanic sunk slowly amid a chorus of heart-wrenching screams from the desperate passengers. We rowed the lifeboat for three or four hours in the freezing cold until the Carpathia rescued us.

Max Staehlin, Colonel Simonius, Max Frœlicher, and their wives survived the tragedy. Mr. Staehlin stated in the article that while onboard he remembered a sudden drop in temperature and a white mass that appeared outside the porthole. It was then that he realized the ship had run full speed into a mammoth iceberg.

A father from a nearby town was informed that his 24-year-old son, a pastry chef, was not on the list of the survivors. My family was sad to learn that. Seventeen Swiss passengers were unaccounted for.

~ 3 ~

As spring turned to summer, I settled into the neighborhood and was getting to know my neighbors. One of them was the Pillonel family, who has a mill. It's on the other side of Route de la Gare and from my northeast side, I can see it very well. Between the Pillonel mill and me is a lush green pasture with a herd of black and white cows.

"The mill is powered by a water wheel," Monsieur Pillonel told us when he visited. "It operated throughout the Middle Ages, as early as 1343. Millers and factory owners obtained the authorization of the ruling aristocracy in 1580 to deviate the course of the Bainoz torrent. When this ambitious project was completed, enough water arrived in our town to run the mill."

The mill changed hands thirteen years ago. Hippolyte Pillonel of Seiry bought it, along with two pairs of millstones. It's now known as the Moulin Pillonel and our neighbor is rightly proud of it.

Our neighbor was still with us when the driver of the postal coach who covered the route from Cheyres stopped in. He told us about a chamois that had made his home in the woods on the Col de Cheyres. He saw it when he drove over the pass. I possess no information about chamois. I assume it's a wild animal and unlikely to come trotting down Avenue de la Gare. Some pieces of information take a long time to reach me.

A year had passed since my family moved into my rooms. The 1913 Almanach des Postes et des Télégraphes was now on my kitchen wall and listed all the Catholic holidays. Our Wednesday market, fairs, concerts, plays at the casino, bingos, and family birthdays were penciled in. Being a newcomer in town, there was a lot for me to learn about the local customs, many of them observed since the Middle Ages. Mysterious notations on the calendar referred to The Bastians, Surrexit, Fête de Dieu, Bénédiction des bateaux, Bénichon, Recrotzon, and the Catherinettes. I looked forward to learning about these local traditions.

The first one I was to experience was Surrexit, an ancient, enigmatic custom that fell on March 23rd that year. There was a lot of talk about it in the house. At midnight, the Saturday before Easter, while our city was plunged into a deep sleep, the twelfth stroke of midnight sounded. Fifty men lit their torches and started off at a brisk pace from the Church of St. Laurent. Easter was early that year and the wind passing over the snow-covered Jura plateau was freezing cold. Nothing, however, would prevent the local population from observing the ancient tradition of Surrexit. Ours is one of the rare medieval cities still observing this mysterious rite. Our parish records show that it was being celebrated as early as 1637. The procession of men from the parish (only men participate) marched off accompanied by musicians, singing in a loud voice to announce the resurrection of Christ. The procession stopped first at the chapel of the convent of the Dominicans where, accompanied by the nuns, the Regina coeli was sung, then to the cemetery where they stopped at the tomb of the last citizen buried. The final stop was the Institute of the Sacred Heart, after which the participants went back to the church to enjoy hot refreshments offered by the parish. My boys will no doubt participate in this ritual when they are older.

The Journal urged parents to warn their children of the dangers of motor vehicles. On Avenue de la Gare, I watched in horror as two adventurous boys hung onto a truck from the Hinderer company of Yverdon. When the truck accelerated, they had to jump off or go to Yverdon. The Journal said that one, the Andrey boy, was not hurt but the other, the Dumoulin boy, was treated for a concussion. My boys were instructed by their mother to be careful of automobiles because anybody could drive one, whether they were skilled at it or not.

There weren't many automobiles on the road back then. At least, I hadn't seen many on Avenue de la Gare, but apparently, there were enough to have a collision. The Journal d'Estavayer was now including photographs in its articles and showed pictures of two automobiles that ran into each other on the Col de Cheyres. I thought it was amusing that horses had to be brought in to tow them away.

Naturally, my boys were fascinated by motorcars, and in those days, no two were alike. They cut out pictures of automobiles and piled up magazines with articles about them. It allowed me to become well-informed on the subject. Firms like Piccard-Pictet, Martini, Saurer, Dufaux,

Les deux voitures automobiles, après la collision

Photo R. Stucky

Berna, and others in the Swiss automobile industry produced some remarkable models.

At a time when all European automobile manufacturers produced cars that were started by turning a crank, Ajax in Zurich unveiled an astonishing innovation. The engine was started by simply stepping on the running board. Unfortunately, running boards disappeared with time and this ingenious starter along with them.

Automobiles Martini SA had been founded in 1904 in Saint-Blaise on the north end of Lake Neuchâtel. The sons of Friedrich von Martini built not only a factory but also houses with gardens for their 450 workers. The settlement was known as Martini City. Neuchâtel had been chosen by the firm for reasons of language and culture. Most of the engineers were French. The firm not only manufactured for the Swiss market but also exported cars to France, England, Russia, North and South America, New Zealand, and Egypt. Two thousand vehicles came off their assembly line, the largest production by a Swiss auto manufacturer. I didn't know it at that time, but the von Martini family were destined to cross my path again nearly a hundred years later.

Naturally, being located directly on Avenue de la Gare, I eventually developed an interest in this new phenomenon of automobiles. In 1913, the industry was doing well. There were about 5200 automobiles in circulation in Switzerland, 1629 were Swiss-made. The Geneva-based Piccard-Pictet produced the Pic-Pic destined to become famous in auto racing. It attained a speed of 180 km in the Grand Prix of 1914 held in Lyon. Of all the Swiss models who competed in automobile racing in the early 1900s, it was the Dufaux brothers' that held the overall record.

The news of the automobile industry was eclipsed that year by the arrival of the first electric train. A picture of the powerful 2500 horsepower locomotive that had replaced the steam train on the Bern-Lötschberg-Simplon line was on the front page of every newspaper. Our country was far ahead of other European countries in electric trains. Our town was looking forward to getting its own electric train. Last week, a boat being transported between Cheyres and Estavayer caught on fire because of sparks from the locomotive. Accidents like that would be avoided in the future when we had our electric train.

Electric automobiles, on the other hand, were set back that year by the American entrepreneur Henry Ford. The *Illustration* magazine had a picture of his assembly line for the mass production of automobiles, reducing the assembly time from 12 hours to 2 hours and 30 minutes. Gasoline-powered cars would now become inexpensive and available to almost everyone. Reflecting on the cloud of smoke left behind by the few automobiles passing on Avenue de la Gare, I wondered about the consequences of a proliferation of gasoline-powered motorcars. I noticed the smudges left by their exhaust on my pristine façade.

A hundred more years would pass before automobile manufactures would turn back to electric automobiles; the gasoline-powered ones having created an intolerable level of pollution.

Although most of the newspaper articles were about cars and trains, among them were some troubling commentaries written by people who heard the distant rumble of war. After two decades of peace, surely our European neighbors had now settled down to a harmonious relationship... hadn't they?

Our annual fair was held from the 6th to the 13th of August. It was an elaborate market covering all the streets of the town center with stands and booths selling cows, horses, sheep, goats, donkeys, mules, pigs, and chickens, as well as cloth, silk, tapestry, furniture, toys, clothes, perfume and miracle cures. The cattle were lined up on the street next to the castle. A variety of performers, freak shows, musicians, pickpockets, and minor criminals mingled among the local population. Merchants came from as far away as France, Germany, and Italy. Our cobblestone streets rang with laughter, music, and dancing. The aroma of whole pigs turning on a spit filled the town center and competed with the smells of manure and sweaty dancers.

Our servants went to the market to buy supplies. They brought back a new steamboat schedule and some strange news. A steamboat operated between Neuchâtel and Estavayer to allow merchants from Neuchâtel to come to our town and cattle to be transported. For the first time, the cattle fair was being held without cows because of the hoof-and-mouth disease, a very contagious illness. Our authorities were concerned that the health measures taken by our neighboring state might not be sufficient. Our local businesses were the first to feel the effects of this disastrous disease and lost considerable custom because of it.

My boys didn't go to the fair. The sun was barely up when they were already sitting in front of their porcelain bowls of porridge at the breakfast table. Milk had already been delivered, brought into the kitchen and the cream skimmed off the top to make butter. It was a special day for the boys and as soon as they finished their breakfast, they scampered off to join a group of children going down Avenue de la Gare.

The starting point of this promenade was the Institute Stavia. The children hiked past my gate on their way to Font. I was worried. Being embedded deep in the ground as I am, I'm sensitive to the most imperceptible of atmospheric changes. There's a treacherous wind on Lake Neuchâtel called the Joran. It can produce a condition called a *Coup de Joran*, that on a lovely calm summer day comes thundering down the face of the Jura plateau with the intensity of an avalanche. My façade had already reached a temperature that prophesied a *Coup de Joran* for today.

I was relieved to see two instructors follow the last of the passing boys. I could only hope they were sufficiently aware of this anomaly and would get the boys to shelter in time. The *Coup de Joran* struck with its usual tree-bending intensity and at the end of the day, while our gardener collected scattered branches and garden furniture, I watched anxiously for the return of the boys. I learned from later conversations that one of them had fallen into the lake and had to be pulled out with a long pole. Along with their mother, I was relieved to see them coming back toward town. They passed my gate post, wet and tired but unhurt and in good humor.

To take my mind off the Joran that afternoon, I looked over the shoulder of the cook who was reading the newspaper in the kitchen and saw that Kaiser Wilhelm II of Germany was coming to Switzerland on September 3rd. He was arriving in Basel with his imperial train at 3.35 and would continue on to Zurich to meet with our Federal Council. The press had published warnings of the hostile attitude and political posturing of our neighboring countries. I wondered why this meeting was taking place. I would have liked to know more, but the cook threw the newspaper into a drawer and hurried to make supper for the hungry boys returning from their adventure. A lot of new things were happening in town including silent movies accompanied by music at the Casino-Theatre. This new experiment seemed to be popular with families. Telephone switchboard hours at the central office had been extended from seven in the morning to nine in the evening without interruption. People were spending more time on the telephone and my family was no exception. Since I could only hear one side of their telephone conversations, I quickly lost interest and turned back to my surveillance of the railway station, where I witnessed a terrible accident.

Samuel Schwaab, a local man, was crossing the railroad track near the Moulin Pillonel. It was raining and he was hidden under his umbrella. I saw a train coming down the track. It was infuriating to be unable to do anything to warn him. Because Monsieur Schwaab was deaf, he couldn't hear the train. The screeching of the brakes reverberated around the neighborhood as the conductor tried desperately to stop the locomotive in time. Unfortunately, it was too late. It was a sad day for the railway station, for the train conductor, and for Monsieur Schwaab.

By the end of November, most of the leaves had fallen and from the temperature of my foundation, I could feel that winter would soon be here. The sugar beet harvest had already arrived at the train station and been sent off to the factory in Aarberg. Some of it now sat on oblong perforated silver spoons placed across the top of glasses in the local bistros. Absinthe was poured through the sugar, forming a perfect mixture at the bottom of the glass. The cedar tree that had been planted last year outside my dining room window had grown two meters and reached the balcony above my dining room. A squirrel had made his home in the tree and was busy gathering nuts for the winter. When he jumped onto my balcony railing, I could feel the grip of his sharp little claws as he walked along the rail. His fur was a pretty red color and his bushy tail was almost as big as the rest of him. I felt I was also ready for winter when my supply of coal arrived from Germany and the reservoir in my basement was filled to capacity.

~ 4 ~

The snow had not yet fallen but a dense fog wrapped around the trees and houses like a layer of cotton wool. Only the blurry tips of the trees and the very top of the towers of the castle and ramparts of the city were visible. Blankets of fog were a common occurrence in our area. On that day, like a stage curtain opening, the clouds parted and the sun illuminated a fairyland of breathtaking beauty. An outline of frost defined the branches of every tree to the smallest twig, the wrought iron contours of my gate, and even the spider web between the bars. A lone blackbird in the park of the Hotel Bellevue across from me, warbled with fervor to call my attention to this spectacular panorama, in case I hadn't noticed it.

It was the third winter since my foundation had been laid and I was beginning to see a pattern in the events that took place around me. Starting with the snow falling, we celebrated New Year's with champagne, Epiphany (also called Three Kings), and Carnival (also called Mardi Gras) a colorful, noisy festival. When the trees start to bud and the *bouton d'or* appeared in my garden, it was Good Friday, the Surrexit procession, and Easter. When my magnolia tree and my cherry trees bloomed, the holidays of Ascension, Pentecost, and Fête-Dieu had arrived. By then most of the flowers in my garden were in bloom and the trees were full of robins and wrens. When my façade stayed warm all night, it was summer. There were grand celebrations on the Swiss National day and the *Bénédiction des Bateaux*, (the blessing of the boats in our port). August 15th was Assumption and my family went to mass at the church. The end of August brought the harvest festivals of Bénichon and Recrotzon. After that, the nights got cooler and the horse-drawn wagons of sugar beets and tobacco arrived at the train station. Toussaint (All Souls Day) came when the leaves changed color and the swallows congregated on the railings of my balconies. We observed the Festival of St-Nicholas when the snow had fallen on my roof and then Christmas, celebrating the birth of Christ. At this time of year, my family put decorations on my façade and in my windows. I supposed it was to thank me for protecting them all year from the rain, wind, and cold. After that, the whole cycle repeated itself.

With the newspapers, journals, and wireless, I was able to stay well informed, even of events taking place outside the country. I knew about the catastrophic accident of the Imperial German Navy Zeppelin taking off from Johannisthal Airfield near Berlin. It exploded at a height of 500 meters. Six passengers crashed to the ground through the front of the gondola. Eyewitnesses said the envelope of the dirigible was completely carbonized before coming to earth, killing all 28 people on board, including the inspector commissioned to certify the safety of the dirigible.

Our newspapers also printed some portentous articles describing the quarrels among the five countries surrounding us, but we paid little attention. Enjoying the sunny days of late spring, we savored our peaceful existence on Avenue de la Gare, blissfully unaware of the ominous storm clouds gathering on our horizon.

The family had just returned home from mass when a neighbor rang the bell. She arrived at the door out of breath.

"Have you heard? The Archduke Ferdinand of Austria and his wife have been shot."

My family was shocked. They feared these assassinations would have dreadful consequences, and they were right. Austria declared war on Serbia, Germany on Russia and France, Britain on Germany. Most of these countries had colonies in other parts of the world that were also compelled to join the conflict. Suddenly without warning, the whole world was plunged into an abyss of death and destruction.

The impact of the war appeared immediately in our daily lives. On my kitchen wall, the calendar for 1914 showed the 8th Regiment of Algerian Zouaves, an infantry unit of the French Army, on maneuvers. In La Liberté, there was an advertisement by a saddle maker, addressed to officers and soldiers. In case of mobilization, we can supply and repair saddles, bridals, and spare parts for wagons on short notice.

News on our wireless informed us that the cavalry had been mobilized in Basel to prevent invasion and the rupture of supplies crossing our borders. Fear of starvation was uppermost in the minds of the government and the Swiss people. Most of our food was imported from neighboring countries now at war. The country had food supplies for only six months. The Confederation bought grain from Germany which came through Basel and Schaffhausen. Orders from America were offloaded in Bordeaux and transported to Geneva. Thanks to the good offices of the French government, most of the grain arrived in Switzerland. Supplies from Italy had dwindled to a few wagons of wheat and corn.

It was still dark at 5 o'clock in the morning when the men recruited from our town filed into the church for a special Mass. They took communion with their rifles at their sides and were admonished by the priest to think first of God, then country and family. At 7 o'clock sharp, the newly deployed soldiers passed my gate on their way to the train station. A crowd of family and friends followed the procession. Many of the women were in tears with frightened children clinging to their skirts. No one knew what was in store for the men when they reached the border. I watched the farewells mixed with patriotic chants, Vive l'Armée! Vive la Suisse! The train pulled out in a cloud of smoke with soldiers waving their handkerchiefs and kepis. A silent crowd trooped past my gate on the way back to town. There was no time to waste on sorrow. Military recruits from the artillery school in Bière were arriving in town the next day. A daunting 320 artillery soldiers and 290 horses needed food and lodging.

A communiqué had arrived in my mailbox for Madame. She laid it on the dining room table where we could both read it. The National Society of Swiss Women admonished the female population to be brave and to take up the duties and responsibilities of the departed men. Their task was to economize food and combustibles, preventing these precious commodities from being too quickly exhausted, and to assume the management of farms and businesses. Women with clerical skills were asked to report to a central office set up to assign administrative tasks. Women's groups took job applications. No matter how terrible and how long the war will be, they were told by the authorities, a lesson in solidarity and helping one another can be learned.

The sun was still high over the Jura when the sound of drums and bugles was heard in the distance. A massive contingent of soldiers bristling with a forest of rifles marched past my gate on Avenue de la Gare. It brought tears to the eyes of the onlookers. The population brought wine and bread for the soldiers tired from the long trek. Three thousand infantry soldiers marched into town and stayed overnight. There was a lot of scurrying around to find barns, hangars, and school rooms to house them. I was able to provide space for many of them and was happy to do my patriotic duty.

The soldiers marched back out at 6 o'clock in the morning, leaving behind them the reassuring impression that our militia was a dedicated and disciplined army capable of defending us against the professional armies of our neighboring countries. The people in town had prepared supper for the tired soldiers and gave them their beds.

I hoped the troop would receive the same welcome all along their way to the border.

Avenue de la Gare had barely returned to its normal state when my boys came running into the hall shouting and gesturing wildly. A company of forty men, commanded by Lieutenant Dubath of the Army Signal Corps, was installing a telegraph line between Payerne and Estavayer hooking up the last link with Fribourg. Everyone in town was fascinated by this endeavor.

"They climbed up the telegraph poles like monkeys," my excited children said. The Signal Corp left for Fribourg the next morning satisfied with their work and their welcome within our walls.

Communiqués from our authorities were appearing regularly in my mailbox. We were informed that stocks of food were sufficient for the moment, but planting was far behind schedule because of the lack of horses. The government warned us that 1915 would be a difficult year and the war could last two more years. The country couldn't produce enough grain for the soldiers at the border, the artillery horses, and the population. Importation was becoming more and more difficult. Farmers were advised to use mechanical seeders to reduce wasted grain. Our authorities were striving to procure seed and horses for the fall work. The army was investigating complaints from farmers that their newly seeded fields were being damaged by maneuvers.

Our government warehouses for grain storage near Mannheim, Germany were now in a combat zone and no longer accessible to us. The government decided to discharge some of our soldiers temporarily to bring in the fall harvest. The work was assigned by the military authority of the local state and included harvesting, guard duty, repair of fortifications and roads. Discharged soldiers held the same status as active soldiers.

I had learned a lot about Belgium because the *Illustration* magazine had a wide readership in French-speaking countries. There was an article in it about neutral nations. Belgium, a neutral country, had been invaded by Germany. It was the scene of three armed battles spreading fear and death among the population. Villages were burned and cities bombed. The events in Belgium had a particular significance to us Swiss. Like us, Belgium and Luxemburg are neutral states under a convention of perpetual neutrality granted by the Treaty of Paris in 1814 and ratified by the Vienna Congress in 1815. It meant that countries granted neutrality did not participate in wars and their territory was not used by those who do. The German invasion of the peaceful country of Belgium was an odious act in flagrant violation of international law.

Would our neutrality soon be violated also?

To reassure the Swiss people, the government made a special broadcast over the wireless declaring that our neutrality would be maintained at all cost. The scratchy transmission blared out the message;

All fit Swiss men are on the march to defend our borders and give their lives, if necessary. The first phase of the mobilization of the Swiss Army, 100'000 men aged 17 to 50, is nearly complete. Our soldiers are stationed along all the borders likely to be threatened, with particularly dense concentrations on the German and French sides.

The government reminded us that our country's control of the major mountain passes between Germany, France, Italy, and Austria strengthened our defensive position and that a Swiss Air Force had been created for our protection.

The antimilitary and pacifist groups who had been critical of our mobilization were strangely silent since the invasion of Belgium. Fortunately, our government refused to be influenced by them and pursued its program of armed neutrality. The Confederation was making a special effort to keep the country united. Given the diversity of our county with four languages and two religions, there was a lot of pressure from the outside to tear us apart and to evoke sympathy for the warring nations surrounding us. Some factions in Germany saw our Swiss German sector as a part of Germany that should be repatriated. The mobilization had already cost 60 million francs and would probably cost 100 million by the end of the year. To meet the costs, a War Tax was imposed on the population.

A heartwarming children's initiative passed from one town to another, starting with the children of Fribourg who took up a collection for the children of Belgium. In our town, toddlers at the nursery school collected 18 francs and brought them to the newspaper office. The Journal published an article called *Bravo les enfants* congratulating our caring children. An advertisement by Kümmerly in the same edition proposed a map of the theater of the French-German war showing details of war zones, forts, camps, etc. It had been published for people with husbands and sons on the front, either duel nationals or volunteers. Interested persons could buy it at the Libraire Butty for 60 cents. In other news, the army physician, whose task was to keep the army healthy, reported eight cases of typhoid, in addition to other illnesses and seven deaths from gunshot wounds.

It was horrifying to see photographs in the Illustration magazine, of the bombed-out cathedral in Reims. The roof was burned, the stained-glass windows smashed, the north tower demolished by a mortar shell, the doorway and statuary reduced to rubble. Being a building myself, naturally, it saddens me when unique and magnificent structures of no strategic value are pointlessly destroyed. News from the battlefront was brought to us regularly by the wireless and our newspapers. An appalling 250,000 Allied and German lives were lost in the First Battle of Ypres in Belgium.

As the disastrous year of 1914 neared its end, the crisp air of autumn lowered the temperature of my façade and the maple trees on either side of my gate post turned a vivid crimson. A flock of swallows congregated on the newly strung telegraph wires on Avenue de la Gare. When an automobile passed or a barking dog startled them, they took off in a soaring cloud. The holiday of Toussaint arrived and the population put flowers on the tombs in the cemetery, as was the custom. That year, an indefinable premonition floated ominously over the venture.

The last article of the year in the Journal d'Estavayer

entitled *Bonne Année* expressed our sentiment at the end of that year.

At the end of this catastrophic year, no wish could be more devoid of meaning, more stupid or more cruel than Happy New Year. While the worst war in history rages around us and our nerves are on edge, how are we expected to be happy?

My kitchen wall now displayed the 1915 Almanach des PTT, printed to raise money for widows and orphans of the war. My children played It's a Long Way to Tipperary on the gramophone and marched around the room. Late that afternoon, an interesting bird stopped for a moment on the pillar of my portico. I knew it was a pigeon; however, there was something strange about its legs. A few minutes later, it flew off. An article in the Journal d'Estavayer entitled *Pigeon Voyageur*, arrived the next day. It read, Wednesday evening at 9.30, Alphonse Kaiser, the game warden found a carrier pigeon at the port. The pigeon had a ring on his right leg inscribed: Paris 03073 and on his left a triple violet ring in celluloid. The exhausted pigeon was turned over to the District Commissioner.

I knew nothing of the existence of a Swiss Foreign Legion. It had never been mentioned in the publications that came to my attention. From my journal, I discovered that this company of seasoned soldiers had arrived in Zurich in answer to the call for military service. The 150 men were the Swiss section of the famous and charismatic French Foreign Legion. Among the legionnaires were men of all ages and walks of life. Some recruits were not fluent in any of our four national languages and spoke only English. Those who had spoken Swiss German in the past had forgotten it and were struggling to understand orders given by the officers of the Swiss Army. One recruit came from Siam and had never been in Switzerland. Despite the linguistic drawbacks, they were a much-appreciated company for their battle experience and excellent humor.

During that stressful time, our Casino-theatre was more important than ever and provided a distraction from the somber events of the war. I saw long lines of spectators waiting to get in for the new play L'Essor. This three-act musical production had some talented new actors in it who had attracted the attention of the population. After the play, a conference was organized by M. Vallotton, a Vaud winemaker, to collect funds for mutilated and blind soldiers on the other side of the Jura. He brought tears to the eyes of the audience with his vivid description of the war just across our border. The price of entry was 50 cents and the collection brought in 550 francs. Another conference was held explaining the new War Tax; how to calculate it and how to collect it. Every township in the district was asked to send two delegates.

The distribution of prizes for the primary school was attended by my boys and their proud mother. It was followed by a charity bingo organized to bring a ray of sunshine to poor families. There were prizes of food and household articles, a blessing for many families suffering from the current economic crisis. The Casino had started holding regular gym practice all year. The authorities stressed that our youth needed stamina to face an unknown future.

"When the war ends, there will be ruins and debts to deal with" they were told.

Our Journal kept us informed by publishing firsthand reports from the battlefront. There were soldiers from our town on the front lines in France. Who were these young men from the State of Fribourg who chose a path of danger and death? Sixty-five of them would never return. They were either dual-national Swiss French, members of the Foreign Legion or idealists who volunteered to fight for a cause. Some were lured from the farms by a quest for adventure, a modest but steady salary, and a promise of a post in the administration of the army after the conflict. One of them from our town, Corporal Vautherin, sent a letter from the trenches. It is reproduced here below as it appeared in the Journal.

I am sending you these few lines to tell you how I spent the Sunday of Pentecost. At 8 o'clock I was sitting in my shelter, impatiently waiting for the cook to bring me some soup and my mail. In this underground life, there is nothing more comforting than news of home, country, and my lakeshore. I heard footfalls in the tunnel shaft that leads to my shelter. It was the cook. He's a little guy but afraid of nothing. He comes with his donkey, loaded with bread and a dozen canisters of soup rolled up in his tent.

"Hello guys, here's the soup", he announced cheerfully. The 'poilus' gathered around him and helped him unload.

"Hey little guy, do you have the rags?"

"Yes, but not for you, Corporal. You have Swiss newspapers."

Soon I was reading the Journal d'Estavayer and finding out the latest news in my peaceful village. Every time I receive the journal, I am both happy and homesick. It has been 15 months since I left Estavayer. I was imagining a stroll along the Route du Port on a lovely evening in May when suddenly, a mortar shell exploded near my shelter and brought me back to the reality of this dangerous place.

We had eaten our supper and stretched out on our camp beds, constructed of boards and gunny sacks. Sometimes a mortar shell gets through the ceiling of the trench and my section chief arrives and yells,

"Everyone out, the Germans are attacking."

We grabbed our rifles and got down in the underground trenches. The canons thundered and the grenades and torpedoes exploded around us. It was total confusion. With my squad, I watched the Germans in case they breached the first line. My lieutenant told me to leave immediately and reinforce the first line of resistance and, squad by squad, we filed through the narrow shaft of the tunnel. The enemy was out of their trench but not advancing. Suddenly, the earth trembled and our front-line fell. A terrifying moment. Those of our men still standing, backed up to the second line in perfect order. The Germans tried to advance but didn't make it because they got a taste of our Jewel 75 (75 mm quick-firing field artillery gun). The shells wiped them out and those left backed up, leaving a pit full of dead and wounded bodies. After an hour of bombardment, everything calmed down. Only a few shots were heard during the night.

That's how I spent Pentecost. We hope that soon our enemies will realize that they can't keep this up much longer. My thoughts for all the friends I left behind.

Corporal Vautherin du 17ème Bat. des chasseurs.

Madame frequently receives correspondence from Jean Ansermet, a friend of hers in the French Foreign Legion. The mail brought a new postcard from him.

Lyon, 31st October 1915.

Madame,

I am pleased that you have asked about me. I had a good trip to Lyon, and I have reenlisted in the Legion. As you see, I have kept my word to rejoin my comrades. I will be preparing for deployment on the French front lines. I leave on Tuesday for the camp of Valbonne. This is my first card and I hope your boys will like the picture on it. For your answer, my address is M. Jean Ansermet, 1ère Légion Etrangère, 5ème compagnie, 2ème régiment de marche à la Valbonne, matricule 36617. Best wishes to all the family. Au revoir if God wills.

More than a year had now passed since this disastrous war began. It was nearly Christmas when I noticed a number of horses congregated on the platform at the train station. Their breath created clouds of vapor in the cold morning air. A small crowd of people had gathered over there. Men were trying to keep warm by stamping their feet. Women wrapped their woolen mufflers closer around their necks and adjusted their mittens. They waited in silence for the train. The reverberation of its distant whistle, once a joyful sound announcing the arrival of students and tourists, now resounded with foreboding. The train slowed and pulled into the station in a billow of smoke. The Red Cross horse-drawn ambulance had priority on the platform, but it couldn't cope with the number of injured soldiers arriving by train. Carried by a stiff west wind, I could hear the words of a doctor pleading with a farmer,

"Monsieur, s'il vous plaît. We need to borrow your wagon. There are too many wounded today."

The farmer nodded and moved toward his hay wagon. Private cars would have been welcome, but they were no longer authorized. Food and gasoline were severely rationed. Volunteers helped the wounded soldiers down from the train cars and carried those who couldn't walk to the wagons. The horse-drawn Red Cross ambulance took charge of the worse cases. A stream of soldiers stepped down from the train, heads bound with blood-soaked bandages, men with severed legs limping on crutches, nerve-shattered young men, boys really, with wild eyes darting in all directions trying to understand where they were.

A local family moved to the last train car to retrieve the body of their son, killed at Ypres in Belgium. One of the many Swiss men killed in a war that wasn't theirs.

The wounded soldiers, a small number of the 65,000 that would arrive in Switzerland during the war to be treated, to recuperate, or to die, spoke French, German, Flemish, Italian, Russian, and many other languages. With the help of the town's people, the wagons were loaded and headed out of the station. The cavalcade of horses and wagons filed past my gate on Avenue de la Gare, bound for hotels and mountain retreats deserted by tourists.

~ 5 ~

On my kitchen wall, the 1916 Almanach had again been printed to raise funds for widows and orphans and showed a convoy of German prisoners being escorted by Allied soldiers. Tuesday was circled in red. The men from our town left again on that day to defend our nearest border at Vallorbe, a vulnerable 47 kilometers from where I stand. It was the third time they had been mobilized since the start of the war two years ago.

The war had created conflicts between our Swiss French and Swiss German citizens. The government was making a monumental effort to keep the country united. Surrounded by nations at war, food shortages quickly became critical. With no natural resources, even in peacetime, we relied heavily on the importation of raw materials to keep our industry going and to feed our four million inhabitants. Deliveries from Eastern Europe were reduced to zero by the Allied blockade and supplies arriving by ship from overseas markets were threatened by torpedoes. The Swiss government negotiated charter agreements under neutral flags to transport goods; however, shipping was often canceled at the last minute because the ships were needed for troop transport.

Our rations of 250 grams of bread per day and 350 grams of flour per month were cut in half. My kitchen vibrated with the sound of slamming cupboard doors as our grouchy cook stomped around swearing under his breath. Rations had also been established for children. My boys were proud to take their part in the sacrifices. La Liberté in their issue of September 28th informed us that the abundant supply of coal from Germany had come to an end. Only limited quantities would be available from now on. My family had a small reserve. I hoped it would be enough to keep me heated all winter.

Another colored postcard arrived for Madame from her friend in the French Foreign Legion. Her face lit up with pleasure when she saw it in the mail. It was dated Wednesday, March 29, 1916, but had only just arrived.

It read:

Madame,

I thank you for the parcel you sent. I was very pleased to receive it. Please do not send any more tobacco because I have enough and receive plenty here. Also, I don't smoke a pipe any longer. I have lost four pipes in five months. I am in good health and glad to see the spring of 1916 which I didn't think I would see, and I hope to see the spring of 1917 with an Allied victory, an end of the German barbary, and the liberation of the oppressed. I cannot tell you where I am, on leave or in the trenches. Speak not! Be careful! Please keep my correspondence secret.

Jean Ansermet

We received some news from the border. The Swiss soldiers posted at the extreme limit of Porrentruy had witnessed a horrifying spectacle. A German patrol of four men crawled along the edge of the forest near the frontier, bent over with rifles in hand and fingers on the trigger. Suddenly they dropped to the ground and opened fire on an approaching French patrol. The wounded French fell to the ground. The Germans got up carefully and approached the victims to take trophies. Suddenly, a half dozen black men erupted out of the forest, chopped up the Germans with their cutlasses, picked up the three wounded Frenchmen, and carried them off. The stunned Swiss soldiers stood rooted in their tracks, moved to tears.

Another postcard from the legionnaire arrived showing a soldier in full battle gear with a bouquet of flowers.

Madame,

I am writing to tell you I am well and that I was pleased to receive your parcel. I hope you have received the cards I sent from Lyon and that you liked them. I am happy here. The food is excellent, but I would like something salty for a change. We have been on leave for some time. It has rained every day since I came. I don't know if we will be here long. I would prefer to be in the trenches in the mud, where we were on our own, although more exposed to danger. I am getting along well with my new comrades, even though they are all new to the Legion. I received a letter from M. Duruz which was a pleasure, and I will correspond with my friends of Estavayer soon. They were very good to me last winter. I hope that my postcard finds you, your brother, and your little boys in good health. I think often of your family and hope to come back to see you. Best wishes to everyone.

Trenches, front line, Jean Ansermet, au Regiment en marche de la Légion Etrangère, 7ème compagnie.

Easter came and time for the Surrexit procession, but our best singers were in the army. The remaining male population was asked to participate in this ancient ritual to keep up the morale of the population. A local soldier wrote from the border:

On the eve of Easter, the bells sounded, and the troops marched for inspection. Two battalions filled the big, beautiful pilgrimage church to celebrate Easter. We had the pleasure of hearing Surrexit and O filii et Filiae sung accompanied by a few musical instruments. The tradition of Estavayer is with us and in our hearts.

It was just after Easter that I had a terrible scare. At 11:34, my foundation shook and my whole structure trembled. I was sure the moment I had dreaded for so long had come; the invasion of the Germans and the destruction of our ancient town. They hadn't hesitated to devastate Belgium, why should they spare us? The first shock passed, and I waited for the heavy artillery to appear. Nothing. No airplanes in the sky, no tanks on the ground. Only silence and clouds of dust. It turned out that we had had an earthquake. The newspaper said it had been felt in all of western Switzerland, but most violently on the shores of Lake Neuchâtel. When the dust settled everything returned to normal. All the same, I could feel a few minor cracks here and there in my structure that weren't there before.

Throughout the spring, there was a lot of activity to observe at the railway station. Monsieur Bourqui of Murist, a soldier in the artillery on leave, came to town with his wagon. I was watching my boys play with friends in the garden and nearly missed seeing him come down Avenue de la Gare toward the station. I was horrified to see his horse fall at the corner of the road in front of the Institute Stavia. The wagon tipped over and Monsieur Bourqui was flung violently to the ground. A farmer with a wagon nearby transported him to the Hospice where he was treated for a broken shoulder and other bruises. He will have to recover from his injuries before he can go back to his patrol on the border.

The same day, I watched another horse and wagon arriving at the station. It brought a colossal trunk of a walnut tree weighing 5600 kg into town. It was bought by M. J. Roget, a wood broker, for 500 francs and delivered to the workshop of the Confederation to be transformed into rifle stocks. Walnut trees were becoming scarce and couldn't be replanted fast enough. Birchwood was being evaluated for rifle stocks. It was lighter, used for hunting rifles, and available everywhere in our forests.

The Monday morning mail brought the newspapers and a devastating postcard for Madame from her friend, the Legionnaire. She didn't know what to make of it.

1 July 1916 Battle of the Somme
I am writing this card to tell you I received your parcel

and wish to thank you. Don't send me anything for the moment. When you get this card, I will be dead or wounded.

May God bless you. A good handshake all around.

Jean Ansermet

An article in the morning newspaper from a local soldier who writes from the front lines did nothing to alleviate her fears:

Coming back from the front we stopped in an abandoned village near the front line of the trenches. We bivouacked in a deserted farmyard and made supper. The fire was lit and the pots boiled and everyone gathered around the fire, happy to be warm and to dry our clothes wet from the trenches. Suddenly the Germans bombed the abandoned village. The sound was infernal. We ate our soup listening to the bombs coming ever closer. Suddenly, a huge caliber mortar exploded over our heads. We dropped to the floor. Too late! A blinding flash followed by an avalanche of rocks and dirt, opening up a crater five meters in diameter. The odor of gun powder was overwhelming. I tried to get up and look around. What I saw was an apocalyptic vision of bodies stretched out as far as I could see, puddles of blood, heads smashed, brain matter, limbs everywhere; blood, mud, and cordite. Of my 32 comrades, 26 were dead. My body survived intact, except for my eyes that were filled with infected puss, which got worse every day. I had to be evacuated. I have been well cared for by the French women at the front and my eyes will soon be back to normal.

Another year of this never-ending war had begun. On

my kitchen wall, the Almanac for 1917 showed soldiers in harnesses pulling wagons. There were no horses in sight. Under its snowy mantel, our little city woke up once more to a bugle call at 5 o'clock. Sixty soldiers from our town were called to the border for the fourth time. At five-thirty, they were kneeling under the vaulted arches of the church, taking communion, their rifles at their sides. At 7 o'clock they marched past my gate in small groups on their way to the station. The train arrived and reluctantly the soldiers boarded the wagons. The convoy pulled slowly out of the station with the soldiers waving their handkerchiefs. The locomotive passed between the trees and out of the city, its smoke leaving long smudges on the snow-covered meadows. Stamping their cold feet, the crowd of parents and friends watched until the last train car disappeared. They passed my gate in silence on their way back to town, as the sun set over the Jura, where our border lies.

Most of the army had been provided with pocket watches, but they were not practical in the cramped trenches. This led to officers purchasing their own wristwatches. By 1916 wristwatches were considered so important that an "Officers Kit for The Front" included a "luminous wristwatch with unbreakable glass" along with a revolver and field glasses. Swiss watch manufacturers had been trying to market their wristwatches prior to the war, but they were not popular with men who saw them as feminine accessories. The new demand from the front line for wristwatches was a blessing for Swiss watchmakers and launched a new trend. Two suppliers to the army, Rolex and Omega, advertised their wristwatches as "Trench Watches" or "Officers Watches."

The Journal had arrived, and Madame spread it out on the dining room table. I immediately saw why.

An article read:

"We are publishing a letter from Jean Ansermet of our town in all its heroic simplicity. Jean Ansermet had been active since the beginning of the war in the 1st Regiment of the French Foreign Legion. He was wounded in combat north of Arras. From the hospital of Poitiers, he sends a detailed account of his adventures to someone with whom he communicates in our town."

You may have read in the press about the victory of the French on the 9th of May north of Arras. It was an honor for the 1st Regiment of the Legion. We penetrated the German defenses and took out 3 lines of trenches, over 700-meter-long, all in hand-to-hand combat. A moment before the attack, the artillery storm was maddening. Twenty thousand rounds of cannon fire from 5 in the morning to 10 in the evening. Everything written in the press about the battle from May 8th to 23rd is true. I saw it with my own eyes. I don't know how I am still alive. Shells were falling all around me like hail. These new death-spreading machine guns are terrible things. Fortunately, we captured about 20 of them last Sunday, which helped us out. I was shot on Monday carrying one of my comrades wounded by a grenade. He couldn't walk and I took him to the ambulance 700 meters behind the lines under heavy machine-gun fire; he was the third one I carried back. I was happy to help and do my duty as a soldier. And I thank God I wasn't wounded more seriously. My wound is not that bad, and I will recover and can't wait to return to fight these barbarians. It will cost them a lot to get me. Those that fall into my hands are finished. My Sergeant congratulated me. I had a nice German officers' helmet I wanted to take as a souvenir, but when I was wounded with my comrade on my shoulder, I had to abandon it. I will get another one. We are well cared for here by the nurses. I go every evening to pray at the chapel and I'm content. When one is idle all winter, you are ready to return to combat and the road to victory. We will get the Boche, it's sure. France still has soldiers and bread to feed them. We will go to the end to get rid of these hypocrites. Please send me a little tobacco, I haven't much left. I lost two packets in the attack on Sunday. They were in my bread sack. The strap broke and there was no question of going back through a hail of bullets to get it. Thank you for your medal. I think it will protect me to the end.

Vive La France
Vive la Revanche
Vive la Suisse, may she stay free a long time
Vive les Alliés, we march to victory.
Jean Ansermet

A few days later, another article appeared and we were informed:

Jean Ansermet of the French Foreign Legion has been awarded the *Croix de Guerre*, a Distinguished Service Medal. He was cited on the French Army roster as an example of courage and valiance. He was seriously wounded while launching an attack on an entrenched enemy position. Congratulations to this brave soldier.

In my rooms, there were tears of relief that he was still alive.

$$\sim 6 \sim$$

The days passed with my children doing their school-work and Madame involved in charitable organizations for the poor and our soldiers. The ladies often met in my petit salon, so I was well informed of their activities. *La Comité de l'Oeuvre des Soldats Staviacois*, an association for the welfare of local soldiers, had so far sent 19 under-shirts, 41 pairs of socks along with a quantity of cigars, cigarettes, chocolate, and preserves to the soldiers from our town guarding the borders. The commander of Battalion 16 sent a letter of thanks to the association for their generous initiative. The Journal reminded the population this conflict would be long and their donations welcome. My boys had each donated 5 francs and were proud to see their names in the newspaper. The second shipment of goods left for the border and was distributed equally among the local soldiers regardless of rank.

While the town was struggling to find men to sing in the Surrexit procession, news reached us from the war front. Easter is a time of hope and we hoped this news would make a difference. President Wilson had asked his Congress for "a war to end all wars" that would "make the world safe for democracy". April 6th, 1917, the US Congress voted to declare war on Germany and called up three million troops. I couldn't help but think of the countless boys, only 10 years older than mine, being sent into the battlefields and the trenches. We tried to dismiss these somber thoughts by listening to our gramophone play Over there, Bring Back My Daddy To Me and For Me and My Gal.

Sunday, August 19, 1917, was a historic date for our small city. No general of the French army was more popular in our country than the charismatic, one-armed General Pau. General Paul Pau came out of retirement to command the army of Alsace. He made it his mission to visit wounded French soldiers all over Switzerland, even the most remote valleys and mountain villages. To the delight of the authorities of our town, a letter was received on Thursday morning telling them that General Pau planned to visit us.

Our town had several of its own fighting in the ranks of the French army, who had been cited for courage and heroism in the line of fire. My family collected up their flags and joined the reception for the General. Swiss and French flags flew from every tower of our medieval city. General Pau arrived at four o'clock at the Place de Moudon, our esplanade overlooking the lake. He received a royal welcome followed by music, speeches, a tour of our castle, and dinner at the town hall. He and his escort left in three automobiles at the end of the day, taking with them the memory of our ancient city and its warm-hearted people. An extra edition of the Journal reporting the visit of General Pau was printed to meet public demand.

On the evening of September 17, 1917, my family and the servants sat around the wireless radio set and listened with apprehension to the address of our state government authority. We weren't expecting good news from the scratchy transmission bouncing off my walls:

"A terrible war has encircled our country for over three years. It imposes sacrifices on all classes of the population, city and rural. The global struggle proves to be relentless and continues to spread. It is impossible to predict the end of it. We ask the population to consume less and farmers to produce products that no longer reach us from outside. Our country has bread for only three months. This year, we have been able to import only small quantities of wheat from abroad, despite the efforts of the authorities.

The Federal Council is now obliged to ration bread. We know this measure will create new hardships. However, we believe you all understand the gravity of a situation created by a war we are not responsible for. The Federal Council addresses farmers to make yet another effort, after so many others. Our State must seed an additional 12,000 poses of cereals this autumn. We address an urgent appeal to our agricultural population to take all possible measures to ensure the additional land be planted without delay. Last spring, you followed our advice and cultivated potatoes and vegetables. The harvest of these products was abundant and has partially insured our supply. Now the country is threatened by a lack of bread. It is in your power to prevent that by sowing the quantities of cereals we have asked for.

So far, Switzerland has been spared the horrors of war. Let us be thankful for this divine protection and accept the shortages before us with Christian courage and a patriotic spirit. We ask, in these harsh times, that you assist the authorities in their difficult mission to ensure the economic independence and freedom of our beloved homeland."

The next day, 1980 bread cards were issued to the population of our town of 2103 citizens. 223 were farmers and made their own bread. My family's bread ration cards were delivered to my doorstep along with instructions for drying fruit, conservation of vegetables, and recipes for jam made without sugar.

That night, a severe hailstorm damaged crops and compounded the already critical shortage of food products. The hail bounced off my roof and gathered in cold little piles on my balconies. During the worst of the storm, the sound was deafening and frightening. There were still hailstones on the streets the next morning making them slippery and dangerous. I watched as horses picked their way carefully down Avenue de la Gare, pulling six wagon loads of straw requisitioned by the army.

The joyless year of 1917 came to a close. Although we had to deal with sacrifices, shortages, and anxiety for our soldiers, we were grateful for the relative peace we enjoyed and celebrated Christmas, mindful of the terror in which most of the population of Europe was living. A wireless broadcast brought us the proud news that the Nobel peace prize had been awarded to the International Red Cross Committee in Geneva for its role as guardian of the Geneva Convention. It was the only Nobel prize attributed during the war years. The Red Cross faced its greatest challenge since its foundation in Geneva in 1859. It dealt with the transportation of wounded soldiers and opened the Wounded and Missing Enquiry Bureau in Geneva to assist families in locating their members in prisoner-of-war camps throughout Europe.

The new calendar on my kitchen wall had a picture of a group of ragged, frightened children watching soldiers march through their streets. Although it hardly seemed possible, 1918 looked like it was going to be even worse than the year before. The steamboat service from Yverdon to Estavayer had stopped. There was no more coal. And since the lake was at an unprecedented low and there were no fish. Ration cards limited sugar, rice, pasta, bread, and coal. There were rumors that the government would issue ration cards for meat, cheese, and electricity in July.

Our gardener said, "We will soon have enough cards to play Jass (the Swiss national card game). Will there be a ration card for schnaps next?" Lent arrived and called for fasting and abstinence. There was no need. With the rationing of everything, fasting was our way of life.

One morning, I was surprised to see a vast canvas shelter that had miraculously appeared near the casino. Everyone in the neighborhood was talking about it. From my second floor, I could look down on the entire structure. My boys and their friends had fun sneaking into it. Our gardener knew all the details and told the cook,

"It's 30 meters long and 5.20 meters wide. It was built by Isidore Torche (a local craftsman) for the American army in France. It has 850 pieces and 230 bolts, and you can put 40 beds in it. It takes four hours and ten men to put it together. An American officer will be coming to inspect it and take it through the border at Vallorbe."

The only good news in our neighborhood was that Hippolyte Pillonel, owner of the mill next door, had been elected to the town council by 188 votes. Madame congratulated him on this impressive score. Monsieur Pillonel's much-needed agricultural experience could now be put to work for the community. Food supplies were the number-one priority. Our government sent a delegation to the United States to negotiate for wheat. The War Trade Board guaranteed the delivery of 240,000 tons from the next harvest. They also agreed to send 30,000 tons of rye, oats, barley, meal, and sugar in December, contingent on the needs of the USA and its Allies.

The men from our town were being mobilized again. This time on the 5th of August. The government was calling up troops from the State of Fribourg and would continue to do so until January. My family hoped and prayed that by January this infernal war would be over. There were repairs that should have been done on my structure, but they would have to wait. Copper, iron, and other metals were reserved for the army.

After the departure of our soldiers, just as the bells of Prime were ringing, a massive hot air balloon passed overhead, barely clearing the lightning rod on my roof. It was carried toward the lake by a stiff north wind. About two kilometers offshore, it plunged into the lake. The Kaiser brothers, our courageous local fishermen, put their boat in the water to rescue the passengers. The balloon, carried by the waves and violent wind, passed offshore of Yvonand where the fishermen, after nearly capsizing several times, came to port. The balloon finally washed up on the beach at Yverdon where it attracted a crowd of onlookers. It was marked with the Iron Cross of the German army. Nobody knew what had happened to the passengers.

On Avenue de la Gare, where there was never a shortage of interesting things to observe, I was surprised to see three tanks decorated with flags pass my gate. With a flair for style, the shooting club of our town had organized a competition for its 42 members. At one o'clock, the club members set off joyously on the tanks for the village of Cheiry, the site of the competition. Our town did well in the competition, especially considering the lack of practice imposed on our marksmen. Ammunition was limited and reserved for the army. Nonetheless, some had to be made available so our young men could learn to shoot.

To my great relief and that of the general population, on November 11, 1918, the bells of our church and churches all over Europe announced the Armistice. The Great War was over. (Later, it came to be known as World War I. Mercifully, at that time, we didn't know there was a World War II ahead of us.) The government authorities addressed us over the wireless. The war had cost 40 million human lives and 1000 billion francs. So much blood, mud, tears, and cries of anguish! Hundreds of cities destroyed, thousands of villages devastated, hundreds of thousands of mutilated bodies, widows, and orphans. I didn't know what to think of it. This practice of war was beyond my understanding.

After the hardships of the war, I longed to return to the peaceful life of our ancient town. I wanted to see people in their best finery lining up at the entry to the Casino for concerts and plays, cattle going to market again, festivals, and dancing. It was not to be. These dreams were crushed by the epidemic of the Spanish flu. This deadly air-borne plague circled the globe and brought sudden death to millions of people. There were cases in the regiments of the army in Valais, Jura, and Geneva and among the population. Rumors that the Spanish Flu had reached our district were rampant. The Journal tried to reassure us. Stay calm, it said, the situation is under control. Don't be alarmed, this illness will pass us by.

It didn't.

Naturally, Madame was worried that the boys would catch the flu. Public events, the casino, and schools were closed. Children had to be kept occupied at home. In the beginning, my boys thought this forced vacation was wonderful, but as the period stretched into a month, they became restless and bored. Emergency quarantine shelters, called lazarets, were set up at the Hotel Bellevue where the Sisters of the Sacre-Coeur received and cared for flu patients, day and night. Every day new cases were admitted from the town and the surrounding countryside. When the number of beds reached 30, there was no more capacity and no more beds. At the nursery, another order of Sisters took in children of infected parents to avoid propagation. The Sisters worked tirelessly to care for the flu victims, giving no thought whatever to their own welfare.

Our church rang the death bells almost every day and funeral announcements filled the pages of our Journal. At the cemetery, no sooner was a grave filled than another one was opened. We learned that in Berne 1200 soldiers were ill, many of them from our district. The Journal asked for contributions for soldiers with the flu and listed the names of the donors. It was difficult to stay informed during this period. Friends and neighbors no longer called. My boys were quarantined and so were their playmates. The local Journal was reduced to a few pages. Eighty percent of the personnel at the printers, Imprimerie Butty, had the flu.

I overheard a conversation in the kitchen and learned that it was known as the Spanish flu because the press first announced it when it reached Spain. The deathly illness had been raging in the trenches claiming untold lives, but the information was suppressed by nations at war, to conceal this strategic weakness. The French thought it had originated in Switzerland, the Swiss believed it came from Germany or Austria, Polish called it the Bolshevik flu, in Rio de Janeiro it was the German flu, and in Senegal, the Brazilian flu. The number of victims worldwide was somewhere between 50 and 100 million.

The quarantine shelter in Estavayer closed its doors on December 20, 1918. It had been open seven weeks and cared for 104 cases. Articles appeared in the journal thanking all those who had cared for the stricken. The primary school opened again to the great joy of the parents and my children settled down to work after their long vacation.

Now that the flu had disappeared, our cattle fair opened again. 85 head of cattle, 275 pigs, and 2 goats were transported down Avenue de la Gare and past my gate. What a joy it was to see this familiar cavalcade taking place once again. I noticed that ladies walking along Avenue de la Gare were now wearing shorter skirts, ending at midcalf, with low waists belted around the hips. They wore elegant winter coats with fur-trimmed collars and close-fitting hats called cloche, decorated with ribbons or feathers.

After the flu epidemic, life slowly returned to normal. I watched as crowds lined up waiting to get into the Casino for concerts and plays being performed there again. Although there was still an acute food shortage, rationing was eased somewhat. Old products came back on the market and new products of all kinds appeared for sale. Rotary dial telephones replaced the old ringer ones and automobiles were again passing in front of my gate on Avenue de la Gare. They were impressive-looking motor-cars called Pierce Arrow, Hayne, Martini, Delage, Model T Ford, Isotta Fraschini, Bugatti, Duesenberg, Stanley, and Biddle. The Swiss automobile manufacturers were dropping out of the market one after another because of the high cost of their handmade models.

To the joy of the local population, our soldiers were starting to return home. One of our neighbors in the Fribourg Regiment No. 7 was discharged with his troop on January 7th. The troop had lost 43 soldiers during the period of deployment. He stopped by to show us the plaque he received in commemoration of his active service. Madame congratulated him for his bravery. In all modesty, he said the plaques were issued to all the soldiers.

We were grateful that the war was over, but the economy was at an all-time low. Because of a cattle shortage, the government decreed that the population observe two no-meat days a week, Monday and Friday. Advertisements appeared in the newspaper for canned fish, canned meat, and corned beef. My neighbor who worked in Cheyres and went over the pass daily told Madame,

"I've noticed the number of chamois on the pass is declining. I only see about a dozen there now. It's not hunting season, but it's understandable that some poaching is going on with so little meat available to feed families."

I still don't know what a chamois looks like.

~ 7 ~

The State of Fribourg came to the aid of its soldiers whose families had been deprived of their livelihood. The 18th of August 1919 edition of La Liberté informed us that an organization had been created called the *Bien du soldat* (soldiers' welfare) and seven million francs had been attributed to soldiers and their families. A lottery was also organized to raise money.

Our Bénichon and Recrotzon holidays were observed with frugality and a meager menu. The soldiers returning from military service had priority for jobs but there were not enough for everyone. The Swiss government tried to discourage its young people from joining the wave of emigration to North America and Australia, promising that things would get better.

There had been a lot of accidental bombing in Switzerland during the war and I was still jittery about airplanes over my roof. At 3 o'clock on Sunday afternoon, an escadrille of airplanes suddenly popped up over the crest of the Jura. In the mist, I could see no markings to indicate who the planes belonged to. The Monday morning newspaper informed us they were French airplanes, nine Breguets and six Spads, stationed at Nancy. Their flight plan was from Nancy to Lausanne; however, because of dense fog, 50 minutes into their flight, they were forced to land near Belfort. When the fog lifted, all 15 landed at Blécherette. I suppose I must get used to airplanes overhead.

As the century emerged from its turbulent teens and the 1920s began, our newspaper was filled with birth announcements following the return of the soldiers, and death notices due to illnesses and wounds that hadn't healed. Other news was the rumor of hoof-and-mouth disease among cows in the region and decrees that shops would be closed all day on Sunday, except for bakeries and dairies. The post office announced that mail delivery on Sundays would be discontinued. Business was starting to pick up and new firms were founded around the lake. In Yverdon, the first Hermes typewriters were manufactured. Forty years later, the firm building them would be the third-largest exporter of typewriters in the world.

To my delight, the vibrant cultural life at the Casino had returned in force. From my northeast side, I could see people coming and going every evening. According to those who attended the comedy Le testament de César Girodet, the play was particularly well done, one of the most successful performances to date. The memories of the painful war years were already fading.

There was so much activity going on around me I could hardly keep up. Behind me, the Casino demanded my attention and in front of me on Avenue de la Gare, another exciting event was unfolding. The State of Fribourg had chosen our town for its annual music festival on the 5th and 6th of June. There were concerts, speeches, and banquets in town but, of course, I couldn't see that. I waited for the parade to arrive on Avenue de la Gare where I had a front-row seat. The first to pass was the soldiers in uniform, followed by the organizing committee, choral groups from most of the villages, children in gym attire, and our own band, the Perseverance.

My very favorites were the Armaillis from Gruyère. Robust, bearded men in *bredzon*, their traditional attire, blue jackets with edelweiss embroidered on the lapels, with a capet (small round skullcap and a *loyi*, a decorated leather bag slung over the shoulder containing salt for the cows. They all carried walking sticks. Their costumes are unique and symbolic of the proud mountain people that inhabit Gruyère. As early as 1840, they could be seen wearing their *bredzon* in paintings of the *poya*, the ritual of flower-bedecked cows going up to the alpine pastures for the summer. I heard that the middle classes in Gruyere had started wearing this costume to church, and the shop selling the costumes in Bulle couldn't keep up with the demand. The parade passed all too quickly and ended with the Fribourg men's choir followed by the entire population of the town. The music festival was a wonderful event I would remember for a long time. The last participants of the parade and all other parades that pass before me, the public doesn't see. Only I do. It's the street cleaners, with their carts, shovels, and brooms.

In the midst of this period of joyous activity, disaster struck. It was six o'clock in the morning and normally I am the only one alert at that hour. Something terrible had happened. A Red Cross ambulance arrived at the Sacred Heart Institute, followed by two others and a crowd of people and cars. The news, when it reached me, was tragic. Five people were killed in a terrible accident at the school. A repairman working on the central heating in the basement wing of the building, accidentally closed the ventilation of the boiler, producing a serious carbon monoxide leak during the night. Three of the workers who slept on the floor directly above the furnace were asphyxiated, as well as two servants whose rooms were next door. Despite prolonged artificial respiration practiced by the staff and two doctors, the victims could not be revived.

Fortunately, the rooms of the pupils and teachers were located safely on the upper floors of the main building, precluding the unthinkable. The dreadful accident was discovered early in the morning. One of the victims must have noticed something wrong during the night because his body was found on the stairs leading to the boiler room, where he was overcome by the gas. Another, who unsuccessfully attempted to open a window was found lying on the floor of his room. The entire city was in shock and extended its heartfelt sympathy to the Sacred Heart Institute. It was several days before our saddened population resumed its normal activities.

Radio broadcasting in Switzerland began on February 14, 1922, with the installation of the first public radio transmitter in the country, just 8 days after the BBC inaugurated their official transmitter on the Eiffel tower. Madame and the boys were delighted with our new invention called a wireless and showed it to everyone who stopped by. It was a medium-sized piece of furniture with dials in the front and tubes on top. I couldn't hear what was being transmitted, but I heard the comments of those who did. Tuberculosis seemed to be a preoccupying problem in France. It was a problem for us also. There was at least one death every day in the State of Fribourg according to the obituaries published in our newspaper. New sanatoriums were being opened, buildings disinfected, and prevention taught in the schools. At the time, I didn't realize the impact radio would have on the lives of my family members and the general population. The tube radio boasted superior sound quality and better reception over greater distances. That year, radio sales in the country rocketed from 980 to 420,000.

The Journal reminded us that the Fonderie Arnoux of Estavayer was one of the town's most flourishing industries. In an interview, the firm revealed their project to melt down and recast a new bell weighing 42 quintaux (1 quintal = 100 kg) for the village of Cormondes. When the bells sounded to celebrate the armistice at the end of the war, the Cormondes bell cracked. Well, it was an emotional moment, wasn't it? There would be a big celebration in Cormondes when the new bell was inaugurated.

It was a joy to see the Hotel Bellevue across the street functioning again. A big blackboard outside the front door described their menu for Sunday, a gourmet meal including fresh fish from our lake, asparagus, lamb, salad, cheese, and strawberry tart for 5 francs. The war had emptied hotels everywhere in Switzerland. The Parisian clientele of the Hotel Bellevue never returned after the war. The hotel published regular advertisements offering cinema and live entertainment and I noticed a considerable number of local people at the entry. However, the vibrant activity that animated Avenue de la Gare before the war was no longer evident. I was worried about the future of my elegant neighbor, but as it turned out, a practical solution was found.

Due to its dynamic management, the Institute Stavia

The Institute Stavia
Photo courtesy of Jean-Pierre Grossrieder

increased the number of its students year after year. The

strict Catholic discipline and intense personal attention given to the students resulted in a high academic level. Parents from the Swiss German sector and Central Switzerland confidently entrusted their sons to the institute.

The number of students exceeded the available accommodations and some students had to stay in private houses in the neighborhood. At the end of September 1924, the Institute Stavia bought the Hotel Bellevue with all of its furnishings. The similarity of the two structures permitted the institute to move in quickly and open its fall term in October with 100 students. The two buildings of the institute, connected by Avenue de la Gare, swarmed with schoolboys carrying books. A constant stream of curly heads bobbed past my front gate

.Since the end of the war, the number of automobiles on Avenue de la Gare had increased dramatically. Because of the train station, the heaviest traffic in the town was in my neighborhood. Our gardener pointed out the different models of automobiles going by.

"That's an Amilcar," he said, as a bright yellow car passed.

In our newspaper, there were ads for used automobiles and police reports of stolen automobiles. The streets near the castle had already been paved and the town council announced that homeowners interested in having the streets around them paved should consult plans drawn up at the town hall. I assumed the streets surrounding me would be paved early on, because of their proximity to the train station. I hoped our authorities would not allow the ancient cobblestones in the old town to be replaced by asphalt.

The pattern of yearly events I had first observed when I was three years old, had repeated itself 10 times now and I was noticing things that had previously escaped my attention. For instance, the food my family ate was not the same all year. Food was heavier in the winter and always hot. Soup made from dried peas was popular, sauerkraut with ham and sausages and raclette and cheese fondue, pot au feu, roasted meat, vegetables, and rösti. For New Years, there was foie gras and smoked salmon and for the Feast of the Epiphany on January 6th, a special three-kings cake was made with a small porcelain figurine baked into it. The person finding the figure was given a paper crown and named King or Queen for the day.

Spring and summer brought lighter and cooler dishes. There was often fresh fish from our lake, small perch filets, a local specialty. Salads and vegetables came from our garden. June brought wonderful cherries from our trees, made into tarts and clafoutis. Summer promised picnics and ice cream. When the celebration of August 1st, the Swiss National day, came around, the population ate cervelas and white veal sausages with mustard served in the streets of the town. The festival of the Bénichon was an enormous feast with ham, leg of lamb, botzi pears, a light bread called a cuchaule (known already in 1558), special sweet mustard, served only on this occasion and only in the State of Fribourg. Dessert was meringue with double cream from Gruyère and bricelets, a flat or rolled biscuit with a pattern on it. A week later, the Recrotzon was observed to eat the leftovers from the Bénichon.

Our servants who did the food shopping at the open market were instructed by Madame to beware of false five-franc notes. She had been alerted that the German government had arrested a band of counterfeiters on the border who had printed 7000 counterfeit notes and put them into circulation. The five-franc notes were among the most frequently used to buy things in town. Everyone was told to examine five-franc notes carefully and not to accept folded bills.

As 1924 came to a close, our economy was picking up. There were pages and pages of advertisements for Christmas gifts in our journal. The local tannery suggested superb furs of skunk, opossum, fox, grey squirrel, groundhog, and cat skins to treat rheumatism. Among the locally manufactured products were Hermes typewriters from Yverdon, clocks from Neuchâtel, music boxes from St. Croix, and watches from Le Locle and La Chaux-de-Fonds.

The new year of 1925 came in with a bang, or rather a tremor. At 3.46 in the morning in early January, the ground beneath me started to shake. I felt a sharp jolt and a few minutes later, a strong tremor. The earthquake affected most of the communities in our district, but my neighborhood got the worst of it. It was the severest earthquake since 1916 when I had thought we were being bombarded. I hoped this was not a bad omen for the new year.

A lot of things around us were now coming from the United States. My kitchen calendar had another picture of elegant ladies drinking Coca-Cola. On our gramophone and radio, we heard Rhapsody in Blue, Somebody Stole My Gal, Sweet Georgia Brown, and Tea for two. The *Illustration* from Paris showed radios that were more and more sophisticated, electric vacuum cleaners, and an ingenious mechanical dishwasher. Dishes were put in a box, water was poured in and by turning a crank, paddles cleaned the dishes. I was sure our servants did a better job of washing dishes.

The morning edition of our Journal published an open letter to the population notifying them that the stockholders of the Moulin Agricole had voted to build a new mill at our train station. They referred to the rapid growth of their business and said their present building no longer met modern standards and could not be modified. The cost of transport was increasing and would be reduced considerably by moving the mill closer to the train station. The Journal thought this was a good thing for the town and for the development of the railway station. I didn't agree. I could see that our neighborhood was changing, and I looked back with nostalgia on the time before the war when Parisian ladies and gentlemen strolled along Avenue de la Gare. I feared that our neighborhood was being turned into an industrial zone. I did have to give the Moulin Agricole credit for choosing a traditional façade which made the building attractive for a mill and it fit into the neighborhood decor. I was grateful for that at least.

Now that photography had become part of our lives, catalogs and brochures were coming in the mail from other countries displaying all kinds of products at bargain prices. Our servants loved to look at them, which allowed me to do so also. The local authorities warned the population it was unwise to order things by correspondence. The products are often not available at the price shown and the quality is questionable.

Local businesses understand our wants and needs they said and can exchange or repair goods easily. It was recommended that we 'buy locally and support the businesses in our community. The population was told that if they purchased goods by correspondence, our local businesses would not survive. I agreed, but it was interesting to look at the catalogs all the same. Madame was leafing through one when a friend on the newly formed museum committee stopped in for tea.

The new museum was scheduled to open on Sunday at 11 o'clock. It was housed in one of the oldest buildings in town, a customs house from the Middle Ages. The lady bubbled with enthusiasm.

"You've heard of Monsieur Hubert de Boccard, haven't you?"

I hadn't. Madame hadn't either. The committee lady continued with fervor.

"He died in Fribourg in 1908. He was a colorful character, who came from our town and remained attached to it. On a pleasant day, he could be seen strolling down the main street, a tall and imposing figure with a long beard, smiling and chatting with friends he had grown up with. In his will, he left his collection of 130 medieval arms to the town of Estavayer. It consisted of armor, helmets, swords, halberds, pistols, flintlock rifles, paintings, and an armchair. The objects were all of excellent quality and some of the pieces extremely rare."

She told us that sometime after that, Madame Ellgass, a pillar of local society, donated her collection of historic artifacts to the town. Our local authorities had talked of opening a museum for some time, and now it was a reality. The mayor thanked the commission for their hard work and encouraged the population to donate their objects of historical value to the museum. I was proud that our town had its own museum now, just like the Louvre I had seen in the Illustration magazine from Paris. Smaller... of course.

~ 8 ~

Thanks to my favorite servant, who still leaves magazines and newspapers lying around in spite of all attempts to teach her orderliness, I saw an article in the Illustration mentioning that some worrying men have come forth this year. Benito Mussolini declared he was taking over Italy and turning it into a dictatorship, ending free elections. Field Marshall Hindenburg was elected president of Germany and Adolf Hitler published Mein Kampf. We haven't forgotten that these same neighboring countries started World War I less than ten years ago. Surely considering the death and destruction it caused, they won't let that happen again, will they?

I couldn't have missed the news of Charles Lindbergh's first solo transatlantic flight on May 20, 1927. Press coverage was particularly intense. His plane was a fabric-covered, single-engine high-wing monoplane called the Spirit of St. Louis. It took off from New York and arrived in Paris 33 hours, 29 minutes later. Lindbergh was only 25 years old. Several pilots had attempted the Atlantic crossing, half of them had been killed.

International events such as these were immediately

forgotten in the wake of our neighborhood disaster. August 16th, 1927 is a date I will never forget. The neighborhood was barely awake when my walls on the north side facing town felt unusually warm for this early hour. An orange light appeared in that direction and grew steadily brighter. Suddenly to my horror, huge black clouds of smoke billowed out of the house next door and I realized that my neighbor's house was on fire. Their storage buildings were full of dry wood and lumber.

People appeared from everywhere, shouting, carrying water and shovels. It was the first time I experienced heat of that intensity on my façade. Everyone in our house and the neighborhood was out trying to help the Chanez family put the fire out. Even though the firemen arrived almost immediately and poured enormous quantities of water on the fire, it was too hot to be extinguished. They concentrated on saving nearby buildings. The flames wrapped around the entire house and soon only the roof and the charred rafters were left.

I watched in horror as the roof slowly caved in and the entire framework collapsed. Only the basement remained. I felt so sorry for my neighbors. Sparks were flying everywhere and I was terrified that I would also catch on fire. Fortunately, the wind was from the west, which swept the fire away from me. I could hardly imagine what it would be like to be consumed by fire. It must be a horrible way to end one's existence. The fire at the Sacred Heart Institute in 1911 had left a vivid impression on me.

The fire at the Chanez family's house had been started by children playing with matches in the attic of the building. I didn't want a new neighbor and I hoped Monsieur Chanez would rebuild the house. And he did, with lightning speed. A few days later, the debris had been cleared away and no time was lost in constructing new buildings.

In the very same issue of the Journal describing the fire, there was the following ad:

Construction Materials & Combustibles
Jules Chanez, Estavayer
Advises his esteemed and faithful
customers that as of today he can
deliver his full range products.
The telephone is reinstalled
Number 54.

A farm building in nearby Cheyres and a building in Monthey also burned to the ground that year. The community and the fire department were doing what they could to combat fire. They organized a demonstration of a new device called a fire extinguisher made by Brulex. During the demonstration, the extinguisher immediately put out a bed of hot coals despite a stiff north wind. It was agreed by those who saw the demonstration that this appliance could prevent the onset of a fire. The state fire insurance recommended that farmers install temperature probes in their silage to prevent fires starting by spontaneous combustion and offered to subsidize the cost. Fire is the thing I am most afraid of. There is little to stop it once it gets started. Fortunately, most of my structure is made of stone, brick, and masonry, which protects me to a certain extent.

Other news in the neighborhood was the extraordinary automobile bought by Monsieur Bovet across from me on Route de St. Pierre. Monsieur Bovet is a cattle buyer. He bought a Martini 4-cylinder TF, on which he installed a large wooden enclosure to haul live pigs during the week. It must have been very heavy because I saw that it took four strong men to lift it. On Sundays, it was taken off and the car transformed into a 6-seater touring car to take the family to church.

Even though I had kept a close eye on my little boys, somehow it escaped my notice that they had matured into handsome young men. They were often away in pursuit of their studies and activities. I felt empty when they weren't in their rooms. My interior was much quieter than it used to be. Henry, had passed his baccalaureate in Business Administration, and the eldest boy left home to take a position with the government. I was happy to learn that Vincent would be staying with me and studying medicine at the University of Fribourg. Our newspaper congratulated the boys on their academic success. Sadly, we lost the brother of Madame that year, only 49 years old. He was a cheerful, much-loved man in town, an active force in the *Chant de Ville*, our men's choir. I would miss this delightful relative, a frequent guest in my rooms.

The neighborhood was growing and the area around the train station was filling in with factories and warehouses. Runways were laid at the Payerne airport making it usable for military aircraft, we hoped we wouldn't need.

From conversations in my interior, I learned that I was to have a new neighbor. A new house was being built on the other side of the Route de St-Pierre. Naturally, I was curious to see what it would look like. It was interesting to watch its progress. The wagonloads of earth carried away by horses reminded me of my own early days. It was a half-timbered structure, with white masonry and dark wooden lattes running through the walls, something I had never seen before. Naturally, there was a lot of talk about the new neighbor. I learned that they were the Borcard family who came from the Gruyère region where this style of house was popular and referred to as colombage.

I had become familiar with most of our local customs by that time. Our town was the only one in the state still celebrating the Circle of the Catherinettes. A ritual from the 15th century. A neighborhood girl stopped in to show Madame her new black cape. On the Eve of November 25th, a group of single girls under the age of 25 meanders through our ancient streets at nightfall. They are dressed in black capes with hoods and each one grasps the hem of the cape of the girl in front of her, thereby forming an unbroken procession. They stop under the windows of unmarried women over 25 years old, form a circle, and sing the Lament of St. Catherine of Alexandria. St. Catherine is the secondary patron saint of the city of Fribourg. The ladies being serenaded throw candy out of their windows for the singers. Whereas only men participate in the Surrexit procession, only young women take part in the Circle of the Catherinettes.

The observance of St. Catherine announced the

beginning of winter and soon it was Christmas. Everyone in the family came home for the holiday. After the sad events of the fire next door and the loss of Madame's brother, we were looking forward to a happier new year. It didn't look like that was going to happen when my 1929 calendar portentously fell off the kitchen wall. Above the month of January was a picture of the S-55 Flying Boat used in the recent South Pole flight. The S-55 Flying Boat was now grounded on my kitchen floor and I had to wait for someone to come along and put it back on the wall. I hoped this was not the omen of a bad year.

Everything seemed to go along normally until July when a terrible cyclone swept through the area, smashing houses and uprooting trees. A downpour of hail and rain washed over my roof and created puddles of water in my allies. The streets were transformed into torrents and Avenue de la Gare was deserted. The wind blew branches off my trees and tore shutters off my windows. Buildings in the surrounding villages were extensively damaged. Entire harvests were destroyed, and barns flattened. A collection was taken for farmers and other victims of the storm. The Journal urged everyone to contribute funds and goods to help those who needed to make a new start.

A storm of another kind happened on a Tuesday in October in the United States. It was the Wall Street crash, the greatest stock market crash in history and known thereafter as Black Tuesday. It started The Great Depression, a worldwide economic crisis that lasted until the mid-1930s. Banks failed and businesses closed, launching a ten-year depression that affected all Western industrialized countries and continued until the start of American mobilization for World War II. Poverty was widespread and soup kitchens fed a large part of the population. As my calendar had prophesied, 1929 was a very bad year.

The calendar for 1930 presented a lighter subject. The LZ127 Graf Zeppelin dirigible advertised regular transatlantic passenger flights from Germany to North and South America. On a beautiful clear morning, I was fortunate to observe this enormous airship as it passed over Lake Neuchâtel. At 11 o'clock, it floated weightlessly over our town, its six powerful motors purring along at low altitude. It was an incredible sight, 235 meters long and 33.5 meters wide. A few small aircraft flitted around the colossal blimp like bees around a hive. Tours were programmed for the days it was in our area, but at 1000 Swiss francs a trip (dinner included), it was not for every budget. It happened that the pilot of the dirigible had a daughter at our Sacred Heart Institute which may have explained its presence in our vicinity.

The early '30s was a time of intense aeronautical exploration. The jet engine and the helicopter were invented. The passenger airline Air France was founded. Auguste Piccard, the first of a Swiss dynasty of explorers, and his assistant Charles Kipfer took off from Augsburg, Germany, and reached a record altitude of 15,781m. They were the first humans to enter the stratosphere. They remained there for 16 hours, unable to find a way to get back down to earth, and finally managed to land unhurt on a glacier. They had been given up for dead. They returned from a height of almost ten miles, shattering every existing altitude record. Professor Piccard ultimately made twenty-seven balloon flights, setting a final record of 23,000 meters (75,459 ft). His study of the stratosphere and ozone was a significant contribution to science. He was congratulated by presidents and decorated by kings. There were two full pages in the Journal about Professor Piccard. I didn't know it at the time, but the adventures of the Piccard family were just beginning.

I had my own mini-aeronautical event when eleven storks circled over my roof looking for a place to land. They finally chose the Sacred Heart Institute and the roof of the Dominican convent to spend the night. In the morning, I watched these huge majestic birds soar into the air and disappear over the ramparts with a grace that human flight had still to acquire.

The thirties were years of change for me. Madame and I were very proud of our boys who had become exceptional young men. They had all succeeded in their chosen fields; government administrator, physician, and lawyer. The reliable family automobile took them on frequent road trips, sometimes as far away as France and Germany.

In spite of the economic depression and rampant unemployment in Europe and the USA, an explosion of new products had reached the consumer market. Advertisements for ballpoint pens, electric razors, nylon stockings, photocopiers, and adhesive tape appeared in my journal. An electric cooking stove and electric washer appeared in my interior. There was good news on the front page of my journal. The war expenses of the military deployment had finally been reimbursed and to the relief of the population, the war tax was abolished.

Our neighborhood took one more step toward industrialization by adding two new grain silos at the Moulin Agricole. The mill at the train station was now capable of stocking 48 wagons of grain. The managers and architects were very pleased with all this. They congratulated themselves on the success of the Moulin and recommended that bakers and farmers buy their grain and flour there. I had to resign myself to the fact that our neighborhood was not headed back to the elegant days of the Hotel Bellevue.

The closure of our Lake Neuchâtel automobile manufacturer, the Martini company in St. Blaise, was the sad news of 1934. Although better built and more performant than other models, Swiss automobiles were too expensive and the local market too small. Our country made intricate watches, music boxes, and high-quality precision machine parts, so naturally, it produced automobiles of the same caliber. As cheaper, mass-produced European and American models flooded the market, the high quality and cost of Swiss automobiles condemned the industry to extinction. Some of the Swiss engineers who had influenced automobile development went elsewhere, such as Ernest Henry working in France for Peugeot and Louis Chevrolet from Neuchâtel whose automobiles became famous in the USA. The firm Sauer built fewer than 200 cars before turning to the production of trucks. It was the only long-term survivor of the Swiss automobile industry.

Meanwhile, other firms around the lake were forging

ahead. Switzerland's precious metal refinery, founded in 1852, became the first Swiss refinery to be included on the London Bullion Market and able to freely trade gold ingots on the international market. The refining company, later known as Metalor, set up a scientific research division in 1938, purchased its first electronic microscope and advanced metallographic control instruments, as well as the first vacuum furnace. Eight years before, it had developed an alloy of white gold and nickel as an alternative to platinum for luxury watches. Dental alloys opened up a new market for precious metals and the company opened subsidiaries in Geneva and Zurich.

~ 9 ~

At that time, our Casino-theatre was bristling with activity. Talking films were the new sensation and had gained immense popularity. The Journal described the first sound documentary; a presentation of world news and an operetta that held the local population spellbound. The projection was followed by the first sound cartoon. The Journal described the joy on the faces of the children watching Mickey Mouse in Mickey's Folies.

Everyone was talking about the unusual program on January 18, 1933. The troupe of M. Glauer, a company of 17 male and female dwarfs, performed Sleeping Beauty. The traveling theater group had played to sold-out audiences in America, Canada, Mexico, and Cuba. Among the talented performers were ballet dancers, jugglers, acrobats, boxers, singers, and musicians, all dressed in rich costumes. Magnificent stage sets had been erected as a backdrop for their performance. They stayed two days in our town and put on a special performance of Snow White, especially for our children. The company of Lilliputians was something unique and would never be seen again in our area.

A long line was waiting to get into the Casino in October. I could see it from my upper floors, and I wondered what had attracted so many people. I discovered it was a film starring Shirley Temple. Every week, this talented little girl attracted more families to the Casino than any other projection. She was acclaimed by moviegoers of all ages. Fresh and tender, with her good manners, kindness, and vibrant health this young girl inspired us all. The Journal said it was incredible how so great a talent could be contained in such a small child. Previews announced the next film would be The Vagabond, starring Charlie Chaplin.

Under the heading Miracle at Lourdes, the Journal d'Estavayer reminded its readers, which included me, of the conference to be given at the Maison des Oeuvres in town on Sunday, April 22nd at 20.30. Gabriel Gargam, whose sudden and miraculous cure had raised enthusiasm for his extraordinary case, was speaking. The derailment of a train where he was a postal worker had thrown him 18 meters. He landed in the snow, his legs totally paralyzed and numb to the point that he couldn't feel a hot iron. Gangrene decomposed his feet, making it impossible for him to move for 20 months, followed by a drastic weight loss until he only weighed 36 kilos. His mother took him to Lourdes. While being transported on his stretcher with a cloth over his face, he came upon a procession of the Blessed Sacrament. The Bishop paused and blessed him. Immediately, he gripped the sides of the stretcher and struggled to rise. He was taken to the hospital where everyone was stunned to see him eat a hearty meal of soup, oysters, and chicken, after which he got up and walked out. He would be giving all the details of his miraculous healing at the conference on Sunday. Entry one franc per person.

Spectators from surrounding towns came to see films and plays at the Casino. A visitor from Morat stopped by to see Madame after one of the performances. When asked for news from Morat, he told us,

"I ran a foot race from Morat to Fribourg this week. It's the first one in the country. It was held to commemorate the victory of the Swiss confederates over Charles the Bold of Burgundy. It retraces the route run by a messenger to announce the Swiss victory."

"That was in 1476, wasn't it?" Madame asked.

"Yes, and according to the story handed down through the ages, after making his announcement he collapsed with exhaustion and died. The branch he carried with him was planted and it is now the linden tree in the square in Fribourg.

I was anxious to know if the young man had won the race and hoped someone would ask him.

"Did you win the race?" Madame asked.

"No. Alexandre Zosso from Basel won it, running the 16.4 kilometers in an hour. There were 14 of us in all. The race is going to be held again next year. I hope to win it then."

He couldn't have known it at the time, but he had taken part in the birth of a historical event. The Morat-Fribourg foot race became one of the most popular and renowned events of its kind in Switzerland.

My new calendar for 1936 had a picture of the Crystal Place, a monumental plate-glass and cast-iron structure built in Hyde Park in London for the Great Exhibition of 1851. It was a coincidence that it should appear on my calendar, the very year it burned to the ground. International news on the radio reported the reelection of Franklin Roosevelt as President of the United States and the appointment of Adolf Hitler as Chancellor in Germany.

These events took place a long way away from my neighborhood and I didn't think they concerned us. As for my own structure, that year brought a Coup de Joran the likes of which I had never seen. I was familiar with this treacherous wind, but that degree of intensity was rare. Fortunately, I escaped with only a few broken roof tiles and was proud to have kept my family safe within my sturdy walls. The Hallwyl steamboat couldn't enter our port and was forced to head back out into the lake to avoid smashing into the rocks along the jetty. It took refuge across the lake at Vaumarcus and finally returned to its homeport. In our own port, several boats broke away from their moorings and were seriously damaged. Inland, logging firms started cutting up the wood from the six thousand square meters of forest that had been flattened.

My family, being devout Catholics, often entertained members of the clergy in my rooms. A frequent topic of conversation was the Swiss Guards at the Vatican. We were particularly interested in them because these young guardsmen were often from families in our town. A visitor from the Vatican told us that Col. Repond was leaving his post after 10 years of service. He had reorganized the

Swiss Guard, transforming it into an elite small army. He installed rigorous military discipline, modern weapons, including machine guns and an ammunition depot. The picturesque striped uniforms, said to have been designed by Michelangelo, had been reissued to the guardsmen who were now up at 05:30 doing tactical exercises. It was regrettable that Col. Repond was leaving his command, due to the difficulty his soldiers were having adapting to his stringent requirements. It will be interesting to hear what the guardsmen returning to our town have to tell us about it.

I may have left the false impression that there are only Roman Catholics in our town. It is true that the majority of the population is Catholic, but we also have a Protestant church. There was an article this week announcing the laying of the foundation for a new church just inside the ramparts, to be inaugurated in the spring of 1937. The Protestant church has been present in our town since 1854. Their religious doctrine is based on the theology of Zwingli, Calvin, and other reformers in the 1500s. Since 1920, they have been grouped under the Federation of Swiss Protestant Churches. Their sermons are given in both French and German.

From the time I was built and began to observe the rooftops of the town, I noticed a white flag that periodically appeared on the dungeon tower of the castle. I wondered what it signified. As I have said, sometimes it takes a long time for information to reach me. An article in the journal brought me the explanation. Since the war, and because of the economic depression, crime had become prevalent and the prisons in our castle were occupied most of the time. In fact, space was often lacking. For the first time this year, the prisons were empty. When that happens, a white flag flies from the dungeon tower. It was pleasant to see, but I doubted that it would last long.

The year was one of considerable change for me. I knew that buildings were often modified and extended, but so far it had not happened to me. My architect, Monsieur Devolz was back in my living room. It was nice to see him again. He looked quite the same. Of course, he was 27 years older and had grey hair. It had been a long time since he had been in my interior and seemed pleased with how well I had matured. He had come to discuss the construction of a two-story addition to be built onto my structure on the north side. Vincent, now a licensed physician, would set up his medical practice in the new addition.

Monsieur Devolz did a marvelous job of matching the annex to my main structure. The same stones were used for the base with carved green sandstone forming the corner columns and white masonry walls. The addition looked like it had always been there. The roof was flat and stopped just above the bottom of an alignment of tall windows in my stairwell. A flight of stairs was added from the parking lot to the first floor.

The only unpleasant part of the operation was cutting openings through my meter-thick walls. Openings had to be made for doors to permit passage from the annex to my existing structure. Doorways were cut next to the kitchen, in the office, and in the basement. It was a strange sensation having powerful saws cutting through my masonry wall and the sudden blast of air and cloud of dust that came through openings.

My new annex

I wasn't particularly worried about it. I was confident that Monsieur Devolz would do me no harm. The door of one room on my first floor opened onto the roof of the annex, which was now a 100-square-meter terrace. There had been an almost unbearable smell of melting tar during the waterproofing phase, but the smell abated as the tar cooled. Monsieur Devolz also designed a well-appointed little garden house close to the new annex.

When the construction was finished, the examination room was tiled, and furniture was moved into the consultation rooms. A large notice was published in the Journal announcing the new medical office opening in the Villa St. Pierre on January 3, 1938. Naturally, along with the rest of the family, I was proud of our new doctor. I was also delighted to see my name in the paper. After years of scrutinizing articles in the newspapers, it was the first time I had seen my name in print.

In our neighborhood, the Institute Stavia was prospering and its academic renown was spreading throughout the country.

Suddenly, in the summer of '39, the Institute was in all the headlines. An exciting mystery was unfolding in our neighborhood. The Institute had been the victim of two unexplained thefts. In May of last year, 1300 francs disappeared from the Director's office. Inspector Marro of the Sûrété had been assigned to the investigation. The criminal had not been apprehended but it was concluded that the theft had been perpetrated by someone from outside the school.

Tuesday afternoon, another theft was discovered. 1800 francs had disappeared from a cabinet. There was no evidence of breaking in. On Wednesday, the State Police and the Gendarmerie conducted a day-long investigation. Suspicion fell on someone who had been seen on the premises on Tuesday. He was actively being pursued by the police. The Journal, known for its optimistic reporting, said he would be caught. I was looking forward to the arrival of tomorrow's newspaper with the next exciting episode of our neighborhood crime thriller.

The Journal didn't disappoint me. New information was forthcoming about the theft at the Institute Stavia. The Police suspected a former student expelled in 1935. His description was given to the Police Monitor and the border patrol. A surveillance agent at the National Exposition of Zurich was intrigued by the unusually large expenditures of a young man at a fair stand. He was taken to the police station for questioning. He gave his name as Dubois from Lausanne. When searched, he couldn't justify the sum of 1032 francs found on his person. Eventually, he admitted to the theft. After being expelled from the school in 1935, he left Estavayer, went to Lausanne, and took up lodging under the name of Dubois. He was in jail while the *Juge d'instruction* completed his investigation. For several days the Journal left us hanging, unable to publish anything else on the case while the investigation was ongoing.

Finally, we were informed that Ernest Riemensberger, a 20-year-old man from the State of St. Gallen, known to the police as Dubois, had been arrested for the theft of 1800 francs from the Institute Stavia. The money still in his possession was confiscated. On Saturday, he was interrogated for several hours by Inspector Marro and finally admitted that he had also stolen 1300 francs the previous May. The method was the same both times. He waited until the teachers and students were in the dining hall, snuck into the office, and took the money.

Once he had the 1300 francs, he took a taxi to Yverdon, a train to Marseille, and a ship to Algiers, where he stayed for a month and a half until he ran out of money. When he was broke, he appealed to the Swiss Consulate in Algeria to repatriate him, which they did and he promptly returned to Estavayer to commit a new robbery. The guilty man would appear before the Tribunal of the Broye District for sentencing and we would learn his fate.

Although it wasn't as exciting, our Journal published what many people were talking about, the change in the weather. Seasons no longer followed their classic pattern and temperature varied enormously. What was causing this climate change? Many people thought it had been caused by airplanes and radio waves, things we didn't previously have. Scientists had not yet been able to give us an answer. In addition, there was the problem of the glaciers receding. In the May 1938 issue of the *Revue du Club Alpine Suisse*, Professor Mercanton published his report after measuring 87 glaciers. Seventy-one of them had receded. The individual glaciers studied showed a reduction of mass from 2 to 119 meters. In the coming years, the population would learn that this was only the beginning of climate change.

While the climate issue was a worry, it was a long-term one. Something closer at hand was happening at the Casino. My family reported that a film featuring the ever-popular Fernandel was followed by one called Our Army, along with patriotic speeches and military music. The film was presented by Lt-col. R. Masson of the Defense Department. I wondered why this program had been chosen. Were the rumors of a new war on the horizon to be believed? I refused to be pessimistic and I turned my attention to Avenue de la Gare. As the sun popped over the Alps, I saw the students of the Sacred Heart and Stavia Institutes skipping and laughing as they passed my gate. It was 6 o'clock in the morning. A special train had been reserved to take them to visit the 1939 National Exposition in Zurich. They were lucky with the weather which was particularly fine. They must have had a good time in Zurich. When, after their long day, they passed in front of my gate on their way back to their boarding schools, they talked excitedly of the wonders they had seen. I envied them their mobility.

Troubling communiqués from our government authorities were starting to arrive, advising the population to stock certain foodstuffs based on experience from the last war. The Federal Wartime Economic Office was reactivated, along with the mobilization of the army. Our authorities feared a new war was coming and were maneuvering to get ready for it. The Wartime Economic Office dealt with provisions for the army, food supplies, and energy production. They had already started working to ensure the production of cereals, milk products, meat, potatoes, fruit, alcohol, edible oils, and other foodstuffs. The journal asked the population to stay calm and to report anyone spreading false and alarming rumors referred to in later years as fake news.

On the 19th of April 1939, in the middle of these foreboding military preparations, the most important archeological discovery ever made in Switzerland took place in nearby Avenches. Two thousand years ago, the city was Aventicum, the capital of Roman Helvetia. During an excavation, a bust of the Roman Emperor Marcus Aurelius was found in a drain. The beautifully detailed bust was made of 1.589 kilos of solid gold. It was extremely rare to find such a thing intact. My Journal printed a full-page picture of it. Copies of the bust were made later for the museum at Avenches and other museums. Although Marcus Aurelius was considered one of the five good Roman Emperors, his reign from 161 to 180 AD, was marked by brutal military conflicts. War appears to be a long-standing tradition among humans.

The solid gold bust of Marcus Aurelius

~ 10 ~

Even the shadow of impending war couldn't dampen the joy of my family as they celebrated the marriage of Vincent, our young doctor, to the lovely Marguerite. If ever there was a marriage made in heaven, this was it. Marguerite was an accomplished violinist and shared the same love of classical music as her new husband. I joined everyone in wishing the doctor and his wife a long, happy life together within my sturdy walls, despite the threatening cloud that hovered over us.

Hitler went ahead with his plans to unify all German-speaking people. He annexed Austria and Czechoslovakia, and on the first of September 1939, he invaded Poland. Two days later, Britain and France declared war on Germany. World War II had begun. I couldn't believe this was happening all over again.

Our government immediately began to mobilize the army to defend against a possible invasion. The country was better armed and better organized than it had been in 1914. The transition into wartime was smooth and less controversial. The entire country was fully mobilized in only three days. There was no panic among the population. It was almost as if conflict had become a normal and acceptable way of life. Parliament selected the 61-year-old career soldier Henri Guisan to be General of the Armed Forces. The experiences of World War I served as a lesson. Authorities immediately put the population on guard against false news being circulated by disloyal residents. Switzerland was determined not to become a center of intrigue and espionage under the guise of asylum as it had been in the last war. Once again, our authorities were firmly resolved to maintain our neutrality. They informed us by radio and the press that everyone in the country must do their part. Those not in military service, both male and female, would do compulsory civil service in the country's interest. This service aimed to provide the country with the workers it desperately needed to maintain the economy, replacing the hundreds of thousands of the labor force drafted into the army. Men aged 16 to 65 and women 16 to 60 without children under 16 were enrolled in the labor force. Everyone was promised a salary.

The peal of the church bells resounded continuously, announcing the new mobilization of our citizen army. Our male population put down their civilian tasks; artisans, employees, farmers, teachers, and medical staff took their oath of patriotism, picked up their rifles, and marched to the borders. Businesses, schools, hospitals, and farms were again left in the hands of the women. When horses were requisitioned, women put halters on the cows, hooked them to wagons, and continued cultivating much-needed food products. Linen, stockings, bedding, and medical supplies were being gathered for the soldiers at the border based on the experiences of the last war. The Red Cross collected mattresses, blankets, pillows, towels, pajamas, medical blouses, aprons, handkerchiefs, tablecloths, washcloths, and chamber pots. The Good Samaritans organization was called upon to assemble the material. They stopped at my door to pick up the goods my family had put together.

Repeated radio broadcasts reminded us that blackout was in force to protect us from night flights of enemy airplanes. Practice sessions had been carried out over the last year. At night, the town was completely dark with a brilliant starry sky. Public lighting was forbidden, and shutters and blackout curtains were mandatory for all buildings. I had shutters on my windows on the ground floor and first floor but not on the second floor. For the windows on that floor, double panels were sewn by the servants from sturdy black cotton with round rings on the top corners so that they could be hooked onto the window frame and be taken off again. Police controlled the blackout and imposed fines for noncompliance. Blackout orders were given in the newspaper and on the radio and were accompanied by air raid sirens when airplanes approached Swiss airspace. Swiss airspace was violated by German aircraft 197 times during the war.

The Swiss shot down 11 Luftwaffe planes between May and June 1940. Adolf Hitler was furious. After threats from Germany, Swiss fighters forced intruding aircraft to land at Swiss airfields. Hitler and Hermann Göring sent saboteurs to destroy the airfields, but they were captured before they could do any damage. Skirmishes between

German and Swiss troops took place at the northern border of Switzerland throughout the war. Basel, Brusio, Chiasso, Cornol, Geneva, Koblenz, Niederweningen, Rafz, Renens, Samedan, Schaffhausen, Stein am Rhein, Täger-wilen, Thayngen, Vals and Zürich were cities and towns bombed by Allied airplanes. The Allied forces explained the bombings resulted from navigation errors, equipment failure, weather conditions, and pilot error. Over 100 Allied bombers and their crews were interned during the war. The United States Government paid 62,176,433.06 Swiss francs for reparations after the war.

Private automobiles were restricted on Sundays. On Avenue de la Gare, a procession of happy pedestrians, mothers with baby carriages, elderly citizens, and nature lovers filed past my gate on Sundays when the weather was warm enough. Even during the week, I saw nearly no automobiles passing on Avenue de la Gare. The auto industry had come to a standstill because of a lack of gasoline. Many owners turned in their license plates, and garages were closing all over Switzerland. The army was worried about the lack of garages to repair military vehi-cles. The federal government asked the states to reduce taxes on automobiles and gasoline to keep the automobile industry alive.

A sound documentary film entitled The Red Plague, produced by the Swiss National Action against Commu-nism was being shown at the Casino. It described the doctrine of Bolshevism and showed scenes from the Rus-sian revolution. Other programs at the Casino included a conference delivered by my own Doctor about gases used during wartime. He left shortly afterward for his military service and resumed his medical practice in my annex when he returned at the end of April. The next film scheduled at the Casino was The Wizard of Oz, starring Judy Garland, and everyone was looking forward to it. It was a welcome diversion from the war news.

Our town authorities, who were themselves stationed at the border, warned us that the war was approaching our frontier. The German Army had already invaded Belgium, Luxembourg, and Holland. In preparation for the dreaded invasion, ration cards were being issued at the Ecole Ménagère, first floor, on Saturday and Monday on presentation of identification. Applicants were asked to respect the posted hours. They were also advised to build bomb shelters in their houses. Subsidies would be available to help with the cost. I didn't think a bomb shelter would be necessary in my case. With my meter-thick walls, I was a bomb shelter. Provisions, however, of flour, sugar, and oil had to be stocked in the cellar.

The Swiss Merchant Marine, the only navy to be commissioned by a landlocked country, was founded in 1941. Its purpose was to provide transportation of basic supplies during wartime. The price of bread went up again. The population was requested to inform the communal office of their current stock and annual consumption of coal. They were reminded that hoarding was punishable by fines.

Notices appeared in our mailboxes calling for young people born in 1920 to 1924 to report for defense lessons and rifle practice. Citizens who possessed arms, gun enthusiasts, discharged soldiers, and members of the shooting club formed up the local guard. Repeated short blasts from the fire horn called the guard to action, and long sounds signaled the end of the alarm. These signals were not to be confused with air alert sirens. Along with the crack of rifle practice at the shooting stands, these familiar sirens became part of the background noise of our daily life. The number of birds in my garden diminished. They had the good sense to head for the forest.

On Saturday afternoon, a mobilization day, I watched a large crowd of soldiers, families, children, and grandparents milling around the Casino. Orders were given, and groups formed up. The bright spring sunshine and good weather starkly contrasted with the dangerous events taking place on our borders. Once more, our people were called to defend our country, and once more, they did it without complaining. It was touching to watch families accompanying the soldiers to the train station, often with the oldest boy proudly carrying his father's rifle. The train station was swamped, and all I could see was a sea of helmets and rifles. Train cars were loaded and pulled out amidst shouts and tears. Departures to the border continued throughout the spring, giving me lots of activity to monitor at the railway station.

The most astonishing thing of all happened on Avenue de la Gare one morning in June. A troop of exotic horsemen passed my gate wearing high white Arab turbans, short red jackets embroidered in black, and voluminous light blue trousers with a wide red sash. This extraordinary costume was topped by a flowing red cloak. The men, their bronzed faces held high, sat tall and straight in the saddle, their leather boots planted solidly in the stirrups. What a magnificent sight! Where did they come from? What were they doing on Avenue de la Gare? I waited for the family to come to breakfast, hoping someone could explain this spectacle or turn the radio on. The cook, always the first one up, watched the troop along with me but provided no information.

The explanation came by way of a patient with high blood pressure who came to see the doctor. More facts were forthcoming the next day in the newspaper and on the radio. Our town was host to 100 Spahis, cavalry troops from Algeria. Their white Arabian horses, smaller than our Franche-Montagne, were nervous, fast, and aggressive. A few heavy Percherons accompanied the troop for moving heavy equipment. They were part of a massive group of 40,000 French, Polish, Belgian, English, Algerian, Tunisian and Moroccan Spahis, along with 7800 horses, that entered our country during the night of the 19th to 20th of June.

The Spahis, providing fire cover for the French Army in advance of the German troops south of Alsace, were caught in heavy crossfire. On the evening of June 17, artillery fire annihilated most of the brigade. Ensuing events in the invasion of France prompted the French army of General Daille to seek refuge in Switzerland. All the troops were disarmed and sent inland. Over 600 tanks and trucks followed the troops. The local population joined forces with the Army to provide food and lodging for this mass of civilian and military personnel. All available automobiles shuttled them inland to lodging in clinics, schools, and private homes. Thursday, the arrivals continued at all border crossings. The interned men appreciated the relative safety and the warmth of Swiss hospitality. One of them said,

"Our guards are very accommodating and provide the required services, but we can feel their no-nonsense discipline, and we know we are in the land of William Tell."

I wondered why these troops were in our country. The evening news on the wireless clarified this issue. It explained that Internment refers to a neutral country's practice of detaining belligerent armed forces and equipment on its territory during times of war under the Hague Convention of 1907. The commentator read the text of the convention.

A neutral Power that receives troops belonging to the belligerent armies on its territory shall intern them as far as possible from the theatre of war. It may keep them in camps or places set apart for this purpose. It shall decide whether officers can be left at liberty on giving their word not to leave the neutral territory without permission. In the absence of a special convention to the contrary, the neutral Power shall supply the interned with the food, clothing, and relief required by humanity. At the conclusion of peace, the expenses caused by the internment shall be reimbursed. The sick or wounded brought under these conditions into the neutral territory by one of the belligerents, and belonging to the hostile party, must be guarded by the neutral Power to ensure they're not taking part again in the military operations. The same duty shall devolve on the neutral

State concerning wounded or sick of the other army who may be committed to its care.

A dozen stables in town had been requisitioned. Our ancient cobblestones rang with the clatter of hoofs as they had in the Middle Ages. No one was indifferent to these exotic visitors, who seemed to have appeared out of The Arabian Nights. To my delight, rollcall took place every night in the Casino square. At first, the Spahis slept near their horses and at the homes of the population during the worst of the winter. The Spahis and the townspeople enjoyed a harmonious relationship with invitations to tea and coffee in the small room converted into a cafeteria on the ground floor of the Maison des Oeuvres across from the church. The young girls in town were particularly susceptible to the charms of the handsome soldiers with their bronzed faces and flashing smiles. A local lady recalls the brutal death of one of the Spahis, stabbed by one of his own over a love affair. The lady said, "I have never seen so many tears flow at a funeral."

General Guisan inspecting the Spahi troops

The internees and the whole town waited impatiently for the visit of our much-esteemed General Guisan. His arrival was scheduled for 10 o'clock. The Spahis lined up behind their officers, made a striking impression in their khaki uniforms, long flowing scarlet gandouras, and white turbans. They had decorated their horses with brightly colored ribbons, braided their manes, and adorned their chests with flowers. General Guisan arrived by automobile from Yvonand at 10:30. He stopped first in front of the Hotel de la Fleur de Lys, where a group of girls from the Sacred Heart presented him with a garland and a speech. Charmed by this warm welcome, he gave the students at the institute the day off. Next, he passed through a corridor of spectators cheering their general and the French Army Chief who accompanied him. He saluted the distinguished commander of the Spahis and his officers who returned the salute standing up in their stirrups. Then, to thundering applause, the Spahis took off at a gallop and passed in review in front of the general. That Thursday morning, the day we were host to General Guisan, will live in the memory of our town.

On New Years' day, the Spahis put on an exotic production at the Casino for the benefit of the public with Moukhala and saber dances to the music of the desert. They thanked the townspeople for their welcome. On January 16th, they marched out of our town and out of our lives. At Marseille, a paquebot waited to sail for Algiers, taking them back to the sun-drenched mountains of their desert homeland, their devoted families, and herds of sheep and camels.

Behind them, they left their beautifully tooled saddles, bridles, burnooses, daggers, and heartbroken young ladies. To the population in our snow-covered little city, suddenly everything seemed colorless, dull, and ordinary. The objects the Spahis left behind are on display in our museum. They are a reminder of those dashing, gallant warriors who raised our spirits that dismal winter.

A stern-looking Marshal Pétain glared at me from the new 1941 Almanach des PTT on my kitchen wall. I suppose I shall have to live with him all year. The population turned to other endeavors and crowded into the Casino to see Fernandel or went to Payerne for the new film, Heidi, played by Shirley Temple. We had a particularly wet spring in 1941. The rain rippling off my roof tiles and creating puddles in my garden never seemed to stop. The marshy land around our lakeshore disappeared under a sheet of water. Outdoor activities came to a halt, and people stayed indoors. With the arrival of the new war, radio sales had exploded, and advertisements for new radios covered the pages in all our newspapers. Radios were now compact one-piece units in attractive wooden cases. Listening to the war news became a daily ritual in my petit salon.

The Journal arrived and had much to say about The Wahlen Plan, a scheme to make Switzerland self-sufficient and reduce dependence on imported food. Friedrich Wahlen, an agronomist, and politician addressed the shortage of resources, land use, raw materials, and food supplies. His goal was to increase land use from 180,000 hectares to 500,000 hectares which he calculated, if accomplished, might be enough to feed our population of nearly four million. Land was reserved exclusively for crops that could be used as food. Public parks, football fields, golf courses, and private gardens were plowed up and crops planted. I must admit that I panicked when I read this. The cook picks up the newspaper first thing in the morning and reads it in the kitchen while drinking his coffee. I wanted to read more about the plan, but he folded the journal and started breakfast. I fretted all day, not knowing what was going to happen to my grounds. I had visions of my well-groomed garden and lawn being dug up and me sitting in the middle of a dusty potato field with carrots pushing up through my gravel alleys. Of course, I knew sacrifices were required for the general good, but would digging up my grounds make a difference?

Instructions were given at a conference held at the Hotel du Cerf. It was declared that all available land must be planted. In our district of the Broye, much of the land is taken up by tobacco plants. I didn't see how tobacco could be used for food. The resumé of the conference in the next day's Journal cleared the matter up.

The current practice is to cut the panicle of the tobacco flower right after it flowers to promote the development of the leaf. This procedure prevents the seed from forming and improves the quality of the tobacco leaf.

Our local Agricultural Office instructed tobacco growers to let the flowers go to seed on a portion of their fields. It was a sacrifice for the growers whose fields had already been reduced for planting food products. It had been discovered that tobacco seeds contained 40% good quality oil that could be used for cooking. The Agricultural Office oversaw the collection of the tobacco seeds and the extraction of the oil.

"Tobacco seed oil!" shouted our grumpy cook. "What are they going to ask me to cook with next, axel grease?"

For our community, a planted surface of 185 hectares was imposed. When non-agricultural surfaces such as gardens, parks, and city-owned parcels were added, the total for the community was 194.24 hectares under cultivation. Much of this result was due to drainage of marshland around the lake, canalization, and cultivation of pastureland. There were also tracts of land that had belonged to the Dominican convent and the Sacred Heart Institute since the middle ages that augmented the tally. We could be proud of those whose hard work accomplished this result despite the lack of farmhands, horses, and resources. This good news put my mind at rest. We already had a large vegetable garden on the north side of my land tended by a member of the household staff, which was sufficient for the effort required of us. In addition, an enclosure was installed around the ornamental garden house for raising pigs, chickens, and rabbits.

On December 7, 1941, my family sat around the radio, spellbound by the news of the Japanese attack on Pearl Harbor in Hawaii and the United States' entry into the war. In European news, we were informed of the detailed plans drawn up by Nazi Germany to invade Switzerland. The adults around me lived in fear and apprehension, not knowing when the invasion would start. In response to this threat, the Swiss military command changed their strategy from static defense at the borders to organized withdrawal to strong, well-stockpiled positions high in the Alps. This military deterrence contributed to the delay of the invasion, along with concessions to Germany and good fortune as greater events of the war focused the attention of the German army elsewhere.

The year 1942 started with an ordinance to reduce electricity consumption. Our post office closed early. Store windows were no longer lit after store hours, electrical signs, water heaters, and radiators were forbidden. Public lighting was reduced by 50%, and private homes, schools, offices, cafés, hotels, and restaurants had to reduce their consumption to 2/3rds of the previous year. My interior took on an atmosphere of chiaroscuro, and dinner became a candle-light affair. A crucial rail link had been severed during the violent battles across the continent, leaving Switzerland isolated from the wider world. To compound the already critical problem of food shortages, refugees were arriving in alarming numbers. We listened in apprehension as radio broadcasts described the seemingly unstoppable progression of the German war machine. Hollow, invisible voices reached us over the wires, enumerating the number of ships sunk, planes shot down, cities destroyed, and the appalling number of lives lost with predictions of worse to come.

For us, it was the darkest period of the war.

~ 11 ~

I don't know who in the family chose the calendars that hung on my kitchen wall, but they must have tired of the depressing subjects of war. The new calendar for 1943 displayed a pretty stewardess from TWA airlines, a relief from Marshal Pétain scowling under the brim of his kepi. The year marked the first major German defeat. The tide of the war was finally turning, though not before 27 merchant vessels carrying precious supplies to us and other hungry nations were sunk in four days by German U-boats.

For some time, a collection called Save the Children had been taken up to benefit children on both sides of the war. Money and ration tickets were collected to provide shelter in our mountains for those needing it. The project got off to a good start when Gottlieb Duttweiler collected two million francs from his customers at Mi-Gros in only six days. Mr. Duttweiler had created a revolution in the food supply chain by fitting out five Model-T Ford trucks and selling six basic products (coffee, rice, sugar, pasta, coco oil, and soap) directly to families at a reduced price.

This customer base proved useful in collecting funds for urgent causes.

It was refreshing to see an article in our Journal that was, for once, not war-related. It was about our Antiphonaries. I may have neglected to tell you about this priceless treasure in the possession of our Parish. The Antiphonaries are magnificent illuminated manuscripts dating from 1480 and 1490. Six hide-bound volumes with exquisitely detailed miniature paintings on vellum pages produced by the Collegial of St. Vincent in Bern. When the Protestant Reformation took place in 1530, the volumes were saved from destruction, and four came into the possession of the clergy of our Parish through a merchant named Jean du Crée. The remaining two volumes were sold in Vevey. The Antiphonaries are kept in a safe place and only exhibited on special occasions under strictly controlled conditions. The Editions d'art at Skira in Geneva published an album with nine of the miniature illuminated paintings from the Antiphonaries as part of its "Swiss Art Treasures" series. It was reassuring in those dark days of conflict that intellectual and artistic pursuits still had their place. The Journal conveyed its warm thanks to the Editions d'art at Skira.

A page out of our precious Antiphonaires.

It was just before the Surrexit procession in 1943, while observing the railway station, I noticed something wrong over there. The afternoon train had not arrived at the station. Two hours later, I heard the screech of metal being dragged against the rails, and at a snail's pace, the damaged locomotive limped into the station. It was frustrating not to know what had happened to it and none of my people seemed informed or interested. The next edition of my trusty Journal cleared the matter up as usual. The two sons of M. Fernand Pillonel, a restaurant owner in town, went to Sévaz to get a steer and escort it to the village of Seiry. On the way, the steer escaped from the boys and headed back home. Arriving at the railway crossing of the Tuillière, the steer was hit by a fast-moving train and killed outright. The boys got off with a scare and a few future nightmares. The train was in for serious repairs.

At that time, we had 300 interned soldiers from Greece in our town. We had had a few problems with some of them going out among the population asking for food, a practice that was forbidden. The internees received the same rations as our Swiss soldiers did. I hadn't seen any of them at my door. Maybe they were afraid to approach me, thinking I was the home of a government official. A notice from Plt. Martin, Commander of the Military Internment Camp informed the population they were not to give food or ration coupons to internees and to report any attempt to sell military boots or clothes. The internees could be used for labor and the population was asked to pay 2.10 francs a day to the city for their services. The city paid the internees 50 cents a day and the rest went to the internment fund. Alcohol was authorized between 12:00 and 13:00 and from 18:00 to curfew.

The Orthodox Greeks celebrate Easter one week later than the Catholics and Protestants. They took a considerable interest in our Surrexit procession and our population enjoyed watching their Good Friday procession a week later. As nightfall descended, 300 Greeks paraded in the streets of our city each with a candle singing the psalms in their language. The last three days before Easter, the Greeks abstain from eating meat. A high church official, Archimandrite Constantin Baliadis, came from Lausanne to officiate and gave a speech praising Swiss hospitality. The event terminated with the ritual of killing a "sacrificial lamb" roasted on a spit in the garden of the Hôtel du Cerf. The Greek internees assembled at the Casino at Christmas, which allowed me to see them come and go. The local population contributed to a lottery to assure there would be a gift for each internee under the Christmas tree. For the short holiday period, our attention was diverted from the war front, where events were taking place rapidly. British and US forces invaded Sicily, Italy surrendered and Mussolini was ousted.

My calendar for 1944 came from a medical supply company, one of many the doctor received in the fall. I guess no one in the house bothered to buy a calendar that year, the fifth of a never-ending war. On April 1st, Schaffhausen was bombarded, killing 39 people and wounding 55.

The Circus Knie, also known as the Swiss National Circus, put their magnificent lions and tigers to sleep because of lack of meat. Mr. Knie responded to criticism by saying,

"Can you imagine standing in line behind people waiting for small rations of meat for their families and asking for 10 kilos for a lion?"

The circus family preferred euthanasia for their animals rather than death by starvation. Closer to home, local travelers noticed the chamois (whatever they are) on the Col de Cheyres were disappearing.

Besides the usual rationing of basic food supplies, soap was also rationed, and using rubber and leather for shoes was forbidden. A small local group of drummers called the *Détachement des Tambours d'Estavayer*, whom we were accustomed to seeing at all our parades, receptions, and military exercises were reduced to silence because they could no longer afford to buy replacement drum skins. The skins had gone from 2.50 francs to 10 and 12 francs. Membership in the group was offered for 1 franc to raise money for this group who was much appreciated in our town and received no subsidy of any kind. The drummers knocked at my front door and all the other houses in town to sell their membership. Naturally, Madame, my kind-hearted patron gave her support.

A friend stopped in to have a coffee and chat.

"Have you seen the Chapelle lately?" the visitor asked. "It's been meticulously restored by the internees from Yugoslavia. It was done under the direction of Sergeant Major Savary. He's such a nice man, so well-liked and very good at finding useful occupation for the internees."

The Yugoslav internees had enjoyed a pleasurable stay in our city and were very popular with the local people.

On the 6th of June, the radio in my petit salon brought us the exciting news of D-Day and the Allied landing on the European continent. There were many casualties during the operation, but the landhold on the continent was a major turning point in the war. It did, however, add new worries for our country as the Allied armies pushed the German forces closer to our borders. The Allies moved quickly through France and in August, Paris was liberated from the German army.

The year 1945 started with the bombardment of Basel, Schaffhausen, and Zurich, killing 16 people and wounding 33, and ended with Germany's final and unsuccessful offensive, the Battle of the Bulge. It was a year of fast-moving events. The massive influx of refugees and scarcity of food compelled our government to close its borders. Nothing could be gained by admitting refugees to die of hunger in our country. The Allies crossed the Rhine and progressed through Germany discovering the horrors of the concentration camps as they headed towards Berlin. Soviet forces reached Berlin, Harry Truman succeeded

President Roosevelt, Mussolini was executed, Hitler committed suicide, and the German forces surrendered.

May is the month cherry trees are in bloom and our countryside takes on the aspect of an impressionist painting. This spectacle of nature always lifted our spirits, but this year it came with the glorious news that the war was over. Around four o'clock in the afternoon, the news that the armistice had been signed was announced by the bells of our church and all the churches in the country. It triggered an explosion of joy. Our ancient cobblestone streets were filled with a jubilant population, cheering and singing. Tears of joy flowed down the cheeks of women whose husbands and sons were stationed at the borders. Flags flew from the windows and draped the façades of our medieval buildings. Schools and businesses were closed. Our beloved *Détachement des Tambours* marched up and down the streets to celebrate the long-awaited event.

World War II, the deadliest military conflict in human history, ended with the surrender of Japan. My family gathered to celebrate the joyous event. I listened in on long and animated discussions on the subject of the war. An estimated total of 70–85 million people perished. Much of Europe was reduced to rubble and its population left without food, water, shelter, or clothes. During the war, our tiny country with no natural resources interned 300,000 refugees, 104,000 of them foreign troops interned according to the Hague Convention. The rest were civilians interned or granted residence permits by state authorities. Of the refugees, 60,000 were civilians escaping persecution by the Nazis, half of them Jewish. Everyone agreed that we were fortunate to be spared the worst of the war. Now our task would be to deal with a nine-billion-franc debt.

I was touched by the prayer of a Greek internee on his departure from our country. Madame sat at the dining room table reading the French translation published by our journal and dabbing at her tears with an embroidered handkerchief.

Thank you, Lord, for keeping me alive,
Thank you, for leaving me among the living,
on those terrifying bloody mountains of Albania
that humans wanted to change the shape of,
coloring them with the blood of the innocent and
littering them with dead bodies.
Thank you, Lord, for the strength to tolerate my
captivity and the courage to cross the border
into the Noah's Ark of Switzerland.
O Lord, bless this country, bless this hospitable land
who opened its arms in my moment of distress.
Continue to protect these pious people,
as you have done so far.
Sustain these people who know how to soften
the bitterness of captivity.
O Lord, you who know the fate reserved for me
You who know the void I have in my heart,
Teach me, O Lord,
Give me the courage to bear my fate,

Give me the courage to rebuild a warm home,
Put before my eyes a loving pious soul,
to comfort and relieve me, to help me be a believer,
Before You, I promise O Lord, grant me this grace
and I shall try to be worthy of it.
Saadi Pardo
July 10, 1945

~ 12 ~

With great joy, I turned away from the depressing subject of war and concentrated on the exciting news about my railway station. In 1945, the long-awaited moment arrived that the railway station would be electrified. Important modifications were taking place. The platform was extended to facilitate loading, new tracks were laid, and the station building itself was transformed. In fact, stations were being transformed all along the line from Yverdon to Payerne. It was a major and costly undertaking. A new schedule came into effect with three trains per day, with a connection from Lausanne as late as eleven in the evening. The Fribourg connection had to wait until the last section was electrified.

The inauguration of the line was celebrated with the arrival of the train at 3 o'clock. Our town band and a group in traditional costumes paraded down Avenue de la Gare to the Hotel Fleur de Lys, where refreshments were served. The authorities asked citizens to put flags on the route from the station to the port. I knew that electric trains were a good thing for the population and the environment. Still, I couldn't help being nostalgic about the billows of hissing steam I wouldn't see anymore, and for a little while, I would even miss the clouds of black smoke that left smudges on my façade.

Not only was the train electrified, but the church bells were also. It was the last time Anna Bovet climbed up the church tower to ring the bells. She did it three times a day, and her arthritic knees reminded her she was no longer young. The last of three generations of bell ringers, she accomplished what may seem like a small task, but it was, in fact, a grand one. It regulated the lives of the whole town. From now on, the bells would be rung by an electric clock.

In this year of transformations, my beloved Casino was also renovated. It was inspiring to watch over 300 people arrive at the inauguration. Our town now possessed a magnificent theater with beautiful well-placed seats for watching films. The excellent acoustics would benefit concert-goers and conferences, as well. Films starring Jeanette MacDonald, Spencer Tracy, Clark Gable, Greta Garbo, and Robert Tylor were enjoyed by the population. Our life was slowly returning to normal. Soldiers were being mustered out of the army, and the local guard disbanded. Behind their enormous flag, the Italian internees paraded down Avenue de la Gare, passed my gate, and assembled at the train station. Our warm wishes accompanied them on their homeward journey.

Rationing was still in place but less restrictive. A placement service to help apprentices find jobs was organized by the government, and a Social Security program called AVS was voted by the people to benefit widows, orphans, and the elderly. Grandmothers were busy knitting warm clothes for war orphans. The population was reminded that metal of all kinds was badly needed and was collected on Thursdays. The population was asked to search through their possessions for anything made of iron, copper, or brass.

With the closing of the borders due to the war, Metalor, the Swiss gold refinery, had turned to producing silver nitrate with a high degree of purity which they used to manufacture fine silver rivets. When the war ended, the firm moved to new headquarters in Neuchâtel to bring them closer to the center of watchmaking. Traditionally, they were suppliers of gold to banks and jewelry makers. They couldn't have known that their move would position them in the middle of a future electronics industry that would be needing a massive quantity of gold.

The entire population of our town participated in a patriotic event in September of 1946 to pay tribute to our soldiers whose lives were sacrificed during the two wars. The event began with a procession of soldiers of all services, officers, cavalry, riflemen, our brass band, and civilian and military authorities. At the cemetery, a wreath was laid to commemorate the fallen soldiers. The Chaplain, Captain von der Weid, made a beautiful and moving speech. The procession then made its way through the flag-decked streets of the town, ending at the town hall where a monument to the dead was inaugurated. I learned about the procession by way of the Journal because the parade didn't come down any of the streets surrounding me. All the same, many of the soldiers came by train, so I did see them arriving and departing.

I mentioned that we have a great deal of wetland around our lake, and a vast quantity of frogs live in the marshes. This, despite the draining and canalization done during the Wahlen plan. When the sun set, it came with an exuberant chorus of riddit-riddit as the batrachians celebrated the end of the day. Between 1853 and 1860, a man from our town named François Perrier* an officer of the Swiss regiment serving in the Vatican returned to our town because of an illness. He was just over 40 years old and was immediately bored with the sedentary life of retirement in our small city. His interest in the frog population took him to the lowest part of the town, where the lake lapped against the foundations of the buildings. Every evening, with his lantern and his net, François Perrier shone his light on the surface of the water. Frogs came to the surface, hopped into his net, and unknowingly embarked on a journey to a strange destiny. In his workshop the next morning, François Perrier performed the minute surgical procedure of extracting the entrails of the frogs and installing wire forms to enable them to assume different positions. He disinfected them carefully and filled them with fine sand. When the taxidermy procedure was completed, the frogs were assigned roles. Being a talented draftsmen and model maker, Francois Perrier built furniture and accessories for his frog figurines. He cut tables, chairs, desks, and school benches out of old cigar boxes. He made dishes from breadcrumbs, soaked in lacquer, and cut uniforms for the soldiers. The stuffed frogs were arranged in scenes imitating daily life in our town in the 1800s. There were students in their schoolroom with their teacher, an electoral banquet with its orator, billiard players, spaghetti eaters, card players, a family dinner, surprised lovers, and a notary public signing an authentic document of the time. All the frogs assumed expressions from real life.

The collection of 108 ninety-year-old frogs came into our museum in 1946. We couldn't have imagined that François Perrier's frogs would be known far and wide and would even become a symbol of our town. Our community museum, having been endowed with interesting historical objects of all kinds since its opening, was overshadowed by the frog collection and became known as the "Frog Museum." The museum, located in the old tithing house, has periodically been reorganized to improve the presentation of this unusual exhibit.

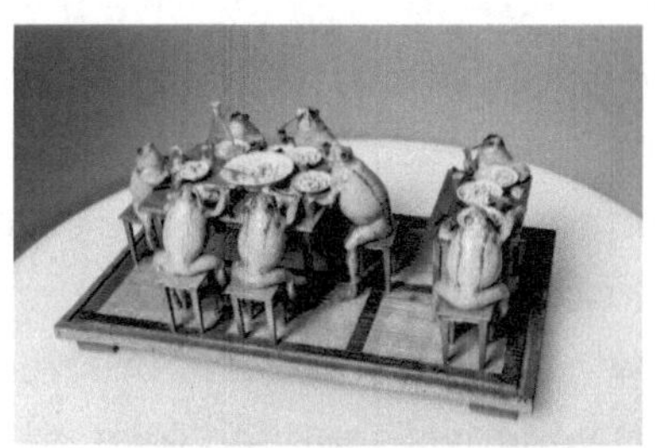

**Courtesy of the Musée
d'Eastavayer-le-Lac et ses
grenouilles.**
Photo by SteinerBrouillard.ch

*François Léodegar Dominique Perrier, 02.10.1813 - 03.09.1860, a second lieutenant in the Swiss Guard at the Vatican. He is famous for having created an exhibit displaying 108 naturalized frogs. It can be seen at the city museum in Estavayer. Source: Genealogical and Heraldic site of the State of Fribourg.

The Almanach des Postes et des Télégraphes was back on my wall and proclaimed the year 1947. What a relief to see a calendar with a bucolic pastoral scene instead of soldiers and tanks. The family had grown considerably, and I experienced the incredible joy of welcoming the newborn babies of my doctor and his wife into my interior. All my rooms were occupied, if not to say getting a little crowded. Henry moved his family and law practice out of my annex to a house nearby, providing much-needed space in the medical office. A steady procession of parents brought their children to be vaccinated, complying with the new law, making measles and diphtheria vaccinations compulsory for children over a year old.

June arrived, and with it, a massive invasion of Junebugs. There had never been a year with so many. Between 8 and 9 at night, I was surrounded by thick clouds of them buzzing around my façade. They made a ticking sound as they flew against my windows and accumulated in thick layers on my windowsills. Madame ordered the family to keep doors and windows shut and turn off the lights. The town authorities tried to deal with the invasion by putting a bounty on the bugs. They paid 0,30 cents a liter for bugs turned in to the town hall. By Saturday that week, 6790 liters of Junebugs were received, 3700 for the day of Saturday alone. Jean Marmy of the Corbière bought in

1630 liters, 100 liters having been collected on just one tree. The new neighborhood newspaper, Le Républicain, housed in an annex added to the house across the street from me, a suggestion that school children participate in the collecting to earn money for a school trip.

I was intrigued by an intensive activity on Route St. Pierre. People had been walking around the lot next to my neighbors, the Bovets, and writing things on clipboards for several weeks. I suspected a building was going to be put up over there. I had seen nothing in the newspapers. If my family had noticed the commotion, they were too busy with their jobs and children to talk about it. It was annoying when the excavation began, and I was still not informed. The size of the excavation was vast, and I simply could not imagine what kind of building would need such a large foundation. I did hope it would be something prestigious like a castle, but that wasn't likely. We already had one. Perhaps a school? We had a primary school only two doors away, and the educational institutes in the neighborhood seemed to be adequate. It couldn't be a family villa like me; it was too big for that. A first-class hotel would be nice in the neighborhood or a concert hall. A luxury hotel had been planned fifty years ago but had never been built.

I was daydreaming of an opera house when the newspaper was delivered and shattered my hopes. The building was going to be a bus depot. Big enough for six buses and two apartments for drivers on the first floor. A disappointing discovery, but I was grateful that the bus company tried to build a traditional building with a style that, according to the Director of the bus company, "would not disfigure the neighborhood." Apart from its size, I suppose this was true. I would have to get used to buses passing along the narrow street of Route de St-Pierre, and I supposed my gardener would have to trim the hedge and overhanging branches. At the same time, the sidewalks on Avenue de la Gare had been torn up to install electric and telephone cables. It was going to be a while before peace and quiet returned to our neighborhood.

An interesting person came my way that year. It was a lady named Jacqueline Thévoz. Born in Le Clos des Roses, next to the bank, she was the granddaughter of the famous doctor, author, and archeological explorer Dr. Thurler who produced the "Vieux Stavayer" performance that made our town famous a few years before I was built. After she graduated from the University of Lausanne, Jacqueline Thévoz, professor of music, composer, and author, turned to choreography. Among her activities in 1951 and 1952 were rhythmic and classical ballet for little girls, performed at the Casino and in my garden. That summer, they were preparing for an outdoor ballet. You can imagine my delight in watching these lovely little girls, one only four years old, in fluffy white tulle dresses flitting through my garden. It was as if a troupe of fairies had landed among my trees. I waited with impatience for every practice session. When the time for the performance came, people paid 1 franc each and streamed into my garden. The spotlight projected on the dancers attracted a crowd on Avenue de la Gare and Route de la Gare, who watched from a distance. The girls danced to music played by an orchestra out of sight under the trees. It was an enchanting, magical moment I will never forget. I owed a great deal to Madame Thévoz. She kept a red scrapbook with pictures, programs, and notes of the performances. She turned up on my doorstep 50 years later and left the scrapbook.

That year, the sad news was the funeral of our neighbor Hippolyte Pillonel, 84 years old, who passed away after devoting his life to his farm, his family, our town, and the district. Monsieur Pillonel had been a tireless worker, a good neighbor, and an exemplary father. He incarnated the solid and dependable citizen, pleasant to meet in his field or across a conference table in town, where his common-sense opinions were listened to. He had been a frequent visitor in my petit salon, and I would miss him. Now, Hippolyte Pillonel rests in the good earth he loved and cared for all his life. His son Henri has taken over the responsibility of running the farm and the mill.

After the war, the method of agriculture changed radically. The horses never came back from the war. Either they were killed, or transporting them was too expensive. The expansion of cultivated land, lack of manpower, and horses resulted in a rapid increase in the number of tractors. On Avenue de la Gare, the wagons of sugar beets going by my gatepost were now pulled by Hurlimann tractors. I missed the horses, but the Hurlimann's had a certain charm of their own and became a legend among Swiss farmers. Tractors were now mass-produced and affordable for almost all farmers. In the Swiss army, artillery pieces previously drawn by horses were now hooked to Jeeps.

I wondered where the fuel would come from for all the cars, trucks, and tractors I was seeing? My dependable Journal brought me the answer. In the Middle East, the fledgling Saudi Arabian oil company, ARAMCO, began producing phenomenal amounts of petrol. A network of pipelines was constructed and eventually crisscrossed the Middle East to transport this product to the end-user. The pipelines greatly increased the efficiency of oil transport, but the article in my Journal wisely pointed out that it also created a dependency on fuel coming from a volatile political region.

For some time, we had been hearing about a new gadget called a "video or television." It already existed in the United States. There were several columns written in my newspaper about this device. It was predicted that the terrifying power of television would modify our social life, sports, and culture. It seemed that nothing was able to stop it. At first, our Catholic church was worried about the mesmerizing effect television had on children. They observed that children in America knew more about Hopalong Cassidy, a fictional cowboy hero, than about Jesus Christ. However, the opinion quickly changed when the Vatican televised a sermon by Cardinal Spellman, followed by a regular television program called Life is Worth Living. Television was then perceived as a way of spreading the Good Word to a large sector of the population.

One of the perverse effects was already being felt in the United States, where television sets increased from 1 to 3 million in only one year. Five hundred movie theaters closed their doors, and it was estimated that most of those remaining would go bankrupt. My greatest concern was the survival of my beloved Casino, where films integrated into the repertory had become a significant part of the weekly program. It would be a shame if the Casino was forced to close because film lovers stayed at home to watch television. The radio industry reported that listening hours had dropped from 3.42 a day to only 24 minutes. Our mountainous topography presented considerable obstacles to television transmission. Antennas had to be installed in remote alpine areas. The Federal Department of the Post and CFF granted a joint concession for television transmission to the PTT (Post, telegraph, telephone) and the SSR (radio). An advertisement in my Journal offered: *A television set on a free three-day home trial. Antenna installed free. Thousands of satisfied customers.*

The time came when my family procured one of these fearsome appliances, and I could see exactly what it was. I was terribly disappointed. What I saw was a facsimile of life reduced to the size of a small window with all the color sucked out of it. Naturally, this was an early model, and as time went on, television sets improved, the color was put back in, and screens got bigger. Later on, I came to enjoy the informative news programs as much as my Journal. The national television programs featured some of our local festivals and traditions. It was exciting to see our Surrexit and Catherinettes processions on the screen. Our ancient cobblestone streets took on a mythic look when they were filmed. The number of television sets increased by fifty percent in one last year. The Swiss French television channels were now available, and I could watch the evening news in French with my family.

Since the end of the war, my existence had been a serene and rewarding one. My boys had grown up, completed their professional training, married, and had children of their own. Music filled my rooms, and the laughter of my young grandchildren filled my heart. It was a time when girls wore flared skirts or sheath dresses and saddle shoes and flirted with young men in leather jackets striving to look like Marlin Brando and James Dean. The world after WWII had changed into a peacetime consumer-led economy with lots to buy and credit cards to do it with.

My doctor organized concerts at the Hospice and with his daughters at the Salle des Oeuvres in town. Everyone appreciated their music and their exceptional talent. I thought nothing could spoil this idyllic life, but I noticed that Madame, my beloved patron, was no longer going to the church every morning as had been her habit all her life. This change worried me. Some electrical modifications had been made to my interior, providing a push-button connection between her bedroom and the doctor's office, with wires going along the hallway ceiling.

Suddenly, the unthinkable happened. Madame, the supreme monarch of our little kingdom, became seriously ill and perished. The family was plunged into a state of sorrow and profound grief. Our newspaper wrote of her spirit of benevolence and simplicity, her dedication to raising her sons, and her religious devotion. It promised that she would be fondly remembered in our town for her tireless devotion to charity and the poor. Sympathy was extended to her sons. On that day, in August 1952, my life changed dramatically. Along with my family, I struggled to cope with the cavernous vacuum, Madame, left behind her.

$\sim$ 13 $\sim$

As it should, life prevailed over death, and my busy young family carved new patterns in their lives and filled my rooms with their intensive activities. There was work to get on with, children to educate, and patients to care for. Our town continued to prosper, and our educational institutes were filled to capacity. The Sacré-Coeur had 252 students, both interns and externs, and the Institute Stavia enrolled 170 students from 18 countries. The Morat-Fribourg foot race had become extremely popular, and this year Pierre Page from Fribourg won it. He was welcomed as a hero on his arrival at the linden tree. In his honor, a 5000-franc prize was created and would go to any Fribourg-born runner winning the race.

The temperature of my façade told me summer was over. My garden took on its autumn colors; bronze for the chestnut tree and burgundy for the rows of hortensias. While the population prepared to celebrate the Bénichon, a smell of tar hovered over the neighborhood. It came from the railway station. The gravel area around the station was being blacktopped. Users of the railway station were delighted with the new surface, especially during wet and snowy weather. The farmers were pleased as well. It made the loading of sugar beets, tobacco, and other produce easier for them. The railroad company had noted the prosperity of our town and the planned construction of a sizeable new canning factory.

The canning factory, founded by the tireless Gottlieb Duttweiler in 1955, was now in full swing with lines of wagons full of vegetables waiting to be unloaded at its dock. The factory management had happily discovered that young men and women from the farming communities around our town made excellent employees. Their sense of discipline and responsibility rivaled employees from long-time industrialized areas. Later on, the Migros factory, known as ELSA, transformed 300 million kilos of milk into dairy products each year. The firm looked forward to a prosperous and serene future and became a vital force in our local economy. Nonetheless, the milk prices they paid provoked heated discussions at that time, even a bomb threat, and continued to do so for many years to come.

An article in my journal in 1955 described a vaccine that had been developed against tuberculosis (BCG). It was offered to the population, free of cost. Our town council addressed an urgent call to the population to be vaccinated. My doctor worked long hours, and I watched a parade of children and adults walk up the stairs to his office in my annex. At nearly the same time, another vaccine by Dr. Salk came out against the crippling disease of polio.

The late 1950s brought us new innovations and old fears. The first computers, modems, robots, solar cells, transistor radios, and videotape recorders came on the market. Nuclear power plants were constructed, and the population developed a traumatizing fear of atomic bombs. On the war front, the philosophy seems to have changed from worldwide wars, perhaps considered too disruptive, to smaller regional wars dispersed throughout the planet.

In observance of our local customs, the Journal d'Estavayer announced that the Sunday following January 20th, the Brotherhood of the Bastians or Good Husbands would celebrate their official feast. It was the day of San Sebastian, the Patron Saint of crossbow shooters. The brotherhood of the Bastians, founded in 1582, originally assembled the crossbowmen of Estavayer. It is one of the oldest brotherhoods still active in the city. To be part of the brotherhood, one must be a man and bourgeois in the city for at least 30 years. The program of the festival includes target shooting, mass, assembly, meals, and a parade to the rhythm of fifes and drums. The procession ends at the Square of the Bastians, where the brothers sing their traditional song. According to the official dress code, one wears a coat and hat, a sensible precaution in January. Confessions are made to the governor of any infractions committed during the year, and above all, good news, such as the birth of a child, is announced. A tax of a few francs is levied on members at their wedding. The day, dedicated to friendship and good humor, ended with refreshments offered by the governor.

The winter of 1960 launched a three-week cold wave and some unexpected visitors. Wild geese from the Russian tundra stopped in my garden and the snow-covered fields across from me to look for grass. Hungry and tired, they were on their return voyage from the south to Lapland and Siberia, with a long way to go. They were welcome to what comfort we could offer them. I was accustomed to seeing an astonishing variety of migrating birds that were attracted by the vast bird reserve on Lake Neuchâtel. It had become a sort of rest stop on the autoroute of their migration. The little black and yellow chickadees that spent the entire winter in my garden had an easier life. Grain was set out for them on the windowsill of my kitchen, and all that was required of them was to add a little color to our winter landscape.

In January, the press coverage was about Jacques Piccard again. His father had set altitude records with the highest flight, and now he did the same for the deepest dive with his bathyscaphe. Jacques Piccard and Lt. Don Walsh of the US Navy reached the floor of the Mariana Trench in the Pacific Ocean. The historic dive received worldwide attention. The descent that took almost five hours progressed without incident until it reached 30,000 feet. Suddenly, the crew heard a loud crack. They continued the dive and finally touched down at 35,800 feet. When they reached the seabed, they saw flat fish and a new type of shrimp. Marine biologists disputed their observations, claiming that no fish could survive the pressure at such depths. Piccard discovered cracks in the viewing window of the bathyscaphe and cut the voyage short. After only 20-minutes on the bottom, they dumped ballast to return the damaged vessel to the surface. I will look forward to the next exciting adventures of the Piccard Family.

I thought my own family deserved some recognition as well. In addition to being a devoted and widely respected physician, my doctor was an accomplished musician. Playing the cello, accompanied by the violins of his wife and two daughters, they formed a talented string quartet much appreciated by the people of our town. I was proud to see the flattering articles written about their performances at the Hospice, the Maison des Oeuvres, and various charity events. I was grateful that the foundation of my family, based on the devoted couple formed by my doctor and his wife, was as solid as my own.

The local population was savoring an era of peace and prosperity. Evenings saw young and old dancing to orchestras in town and nearby villages. When winter came, young people skated on the Grande Gouille, a big shallow puddle near the lakeshore that stayed frozen all winter. Camping had become a popular way of vacationing. An exhibition of Volkswagen camping buses was on display in Payerne. My Journal was full of advertisements for the newest and latest in portable, table and floor-model radios, phonographs, recorders, stereos, and a vast choice of 78 rpm records for children and adults. Telephone calls placed by switchboard operators could now be made by direct dialing, even to nearby European countries.

The funeral of the much-loved General Guisan took place on April 12, 1960. Newspapers, radio, and television covered the sad event. Rarely had a citizen in our country acquired such a deep admiration and gratitude. The population was grateful to him for guiding them through the insanity of the last war. He never failed in his duty to his soldiers, the population, or his profound Christian faith. Because of his visit to our town 20 years ago, our population felt a special connection with the esteemed General and an intimate sadness at his demise. The kilometer-long funeral procession observed by a dense and tearful population arrived at the Cathedral of Lausanne. Among the military fanfare, authorities, and sea of wreaths from Swiss and foreign powers, the most poignant symbol of our separation from this remarkable man was the passage of his horse, saddled and alone, behind the artillery piece carrying the flag-covered coffin of the General.

Turning my attention back to the neighborhood, I had noticed that the bus company next door was very active with its organized trips. It offered bus trips with accommodations to Germany, France, Italy, mountainous areas in Austria, and our own Alps. Paris and Venice were also popular destinations. I had been disappointed at first that this bus station had been built in our neighborhood instead of a more cultural establishment, but I have to admit now that their organized trips did bring a lot of pleasure to the new middle class. There were already several bus companies competing for the local clientele. Regular boat service on the canals linking the Lakes of Neuchâtel, Morat, and Bienne opened up another pleasant way to travel through our district. The authorities informed us that, effective November 1, 1962, visitors to the region would be taxed 0.30 Sfr. per person per night in hotels, pensions, rented villas, and chalets.

Until now, Avenue de la Gare and other streets were used simultaneously by horses and wagons, cars, trucks, buses, pedestrians, bicycles, prams, and dogs. With the increase in the population and the number of vehicles, road accidents had become alarmingly commonplace. My doctor was called out frequently to treat serious injuries. For some time, sidewalks had been under discussion by the local authorities, and when the time came to re-surface the street, they were incorporated into the plan. In front of my gate and along the border of Avenue de la Gare, there were piles of gravel, sand, earth, pavers, and stacks of tools. My days were fully occupied observing this intense construction activity. When my sidewalk was fin-ished (I considered it mine even though it was outside my gate), it was 1.80 meters wide and five centimeters higher than the rest of the road. The surface was covered with 20 mm of bitumen and reserved for pedestrians, prams, and children's tricycles. This practical, raised walkway protected pedestrians and children from cars and trucks. Once the town was fitted out with sidewalks, the number of pedestrian accidents reported in my Journal dropped considerably.

With a touch of nostalgia, I watched the parade of what was now called vintage automobiles on Avenue de la Gare. An international rally organized by the Veteran car club of Neuchâtel passed through our town. A long procession passed my gate and included the venerable makes of Duesenberg, Bugatti, Martini, de Dion-Bouton, Hotchkiss, Mercedes, Delage, Essex, Hispano-Suiza, Isotta-Francini, Packard, and Panhard. When I was young, I had observed these motorcars with their long hoods, bug-eyed headlights, and spoked wheels. They were new, modern cars then, and there weren't many of them. I hadn't realized back then that change was inevitable. Horses were replaced by automobiles, steam trains and gas lamps by electricity, and unique handmade automobiles by mundane production models. For that one special afternoon, however, Avenue de la Gare brought back the glory days of the automobile industry.

I had been looking forward to seeing the total eclipse of the sun that had been announced in the newspaper. Unfortunately, due to fog cover, a frequent problem in our area, it wasn't visible. The Journal advised us to be patient. The next eclipse would be in 1999, a mere 37 years away. Waiting is not a problem for me. The persistent fog we experienced in those days, was a problem for navigation on our lake. A useful system of storm warning lights had been installed around the lake to warn boats of fog, impending storms, or strong winds like the Joran.

The new year of 1964 had barely begun when the death knell rang endlessly from our church tower, its mournful peal floating over the frozen rooftops of our town. It seems that when life is at its happiest and most trouble-free that tragedy strikes. My grandchildren were all doing well socially and academically. My doctor and his wife were busy with musical and theatrical pursuits in our town. I had started to worry when I noticed that the lovely wife of my doctor was spending a lot of time in bed, and her radiant health seemed to be rapidly fading. My doctor hovered and paced and did everything possible to help her recover. As her condition worsened, he never left her side. Only 49 years old, she succumbed to a serious illness, plunging the family into sorrow and leaving an abysmal void behind her. Our Journal reported the tragic news and described the fine and distinguished woman she had been, mother of six children, much loved in her home and her city. The Journal and the population of our town extended their heartfelt sympathy to my doctor, his children, and the family of his wife.

My heartbroken widower carried on as best he could supported by the rest of the family. He continued his medical practice but seemed frozen in the past when his beloved wife was still with him. It was the beginning of my decline as well. The routine maintenance of my structure was done less often. The doctor wanted nothing around him changed. My garden developed an air of neglect. Untrimmed trees reduced the light coming into the house, and my interior resembled the war years when electricity was rationed.

The unhappy year came to a close with Brigitte Bardot's economically clad appearance at the Casino in her first film, And God Created Woman. The young women on Avenue de la Gare were wearing miniskirts, a new craze from London that had shaken up women's fashion. Footwear was leather boots and high-heeled shoes with pointed toes. Little girls carried Barbie dolls. My calendar for 1965 displayed the new Ford Mustang, an elegant muscle car that came on the market the year before.

The tourism industry in our area was being dragged along by the Development Society. Competition for tourists was stiff, and our area had fewer cards to play than the alpine regions, irreverently referred to by our tourist office as Heidiland. In addition, the spectacular vineyards of Lavaux and their breath-taking view of the Dent du Midi were too close for comfort. But our town has never lacked imagination. An ingenious apparatus was constructed on our community beach that spring. It was a nautical ski tow; the first and only one in the country; the second one in Europe. A series of pylons were sunk into the lake. A cable suspended between them pulled a water skier around a circuit, thereby replacing a motorboat. The conversations of the young people in my interior and their friends brought me all the details. One of them had tried it and fallen into the water, where a small motorboat picked him up and brought him to shore.

Our hyperactive Development Society published an article reminding homeowners that our town is known as the "City of the Rose" and deplored the lack of roses in it. The society encouraged owners of buildings in the old town to grow climbing roses on their façades. The population embraced the idea with enthusiasm. It was the beginning of a new tradition. By the end of the century, roses adorned all the buildings in the old town, and a bi-annual rose festival brought rose growers, perfumers, and rose lovers from all over the country. My gardener joined the ranks and decided that a climbing rose would be attached to my façade. I wasn't consulted, even though it was me the plant was going to be fixed to. Naturally, it would add to my beauty, and I wasn't against the idea, so long as a variety was chosen that wasn't going to sink thorns into me.

The same year the Dominican sisters, whose convent was founded in 1316, celebrated their 650th anniversary. The Journal had much to say about the courage and dedication they had shown throughout their turbulent history. Members of their order had endured the plunder and destruction of the town in 1475 by Bern and Fribourg, cared for the population during the plague in 1528, awaited the outcome of the Sonderbund war of 1847, and surrendered to the Helvetic republic. But the most noteworthy event in their history was "the miracle," recorded by Adrien Daubigney in his written history of the convent. The author affirms that he heard about the miracle in 1847 from Rev. Mother Ellie Demierre, 84 years and sound of mind.

The miracle happened on February 11th, 1773, during a period of famine and extreme poverty. A young woman named Chantauroz came to the convent with a small sack and begged for grain to save her family from starvation. The gatekeeper told her it was impossible. There was no grain left, only the sweepings on the threshing floor.

"Then give me the sweepings," cried the distraught young women.

The gatekeeper was touched by her grief and took her to the granary with two sisters. When they arrived, they looked out of the window and saw 32 sacks stacked along the wall of the convent, bursting with top-quality grain. They ran to get the other sisters and joyfully transported the grain, giving thanks to God for this miracle.

Sister Rose Marmy of the Tiers-Ordre, a servant at the

convent, reported the event in 1804, saying she had seen the miracle herself.

A Quotation of Mother Rose Tercier states: *The same narration came from Catherine, daughter of Monsieur Enard, goldsmith in Estavayer and the wife of Monsieur Jordil in 1823, she had heard it from her parents.*

A year after that, a miracle of another kind happened in my neighborhood. Night turned to day.

Streetlights were installed all along Avenue de la Gare and other streets in the neighborhood. It made my life more interesting because I could see people on their way to the train station after dark. The habitually late passengers running to catch the train now had a better chance of getting there without tripping over something. Lovers were not so enthusiastic and moved back into less lit areas. I even had my own lamp post, installed just outside my gate, giving my entrance on Avenue de la Gare a welcoming appeal that pleased me.

My doctor's children were growing up and would soon be leaving me. The tragic loss of their mother had affected all the children, but most of all, the doctor himself. Music still brought him pleasure. His presence at events like the inauguration of the organ at the Sacred Heart Institute and his in-depth commentaries on concerts were much appreciated and often published in the pages of my Journal.

In the 1960s, the coastline of our town consisted of a pier for the scheduled boat service and private moorings for fishing boats. With the post-war economic boom, more people were buying pleasure craft. Fiberglass had replaced wood for boat hulls, reducing maintenance and making boating more carefree. Lake Neuchâtel, with its 38.3 km length and 8.2 km width, the Jura on one side and the Prealps on the other, is a perfect wind tunnel. Our sailing club, the CVE (Circle de voile d'Estavayer), wanted to build a port for sailboats and organize local and national regattas. They obtained a concession to use the body of water southwest of the pier, marshaled their members and potential shareholders, and presented a proposal to the town council. In the council meeting of October 26, 1969, La Liberté quotes the city mayor, who declared the town was fortunate that this private initiative was being undertaken. A building permit for the port was issued. The authorities wished to retain a certain number of berths for the town.

A year later, it was official, and the sailing port of Estavayer was on the starting line. The first step was to acquire the monumental sum of 300,000 francs and construct a 370-meter jetty for the first 100 moorings. Assembling the private funds was a complex affair (a bank loan of 120,000 francs secured by the town helped). The footbridges, clubhouse, crane, and gasoline column would have to wait until more funds could be acquired.

At the inauguration of the port, the Préfect congratulated the CVE on overcoming the many technical and financial challenges. It was the only port on the Lake of Neuchâtel built without the aid of its community. The CVE created a corporation in 1971 to adminîstrate the port facility. Its mission was to make sailing accessible to everyone. Mooring fees were the lowest on the lake, and generations of young people from the area learned to sail at camps and weekly classes in boats provided by the CVE at a minimal cost. The Port of Estavayer and the CVE looked forward to smooth sailing for nearly half a century; they had it.

February is always a dismal month, but in 1971 it brought some good news. Women in Switzerland had been given the right to vote in federal elections by a 66% margin. It was about time. By 1971, only eight states had granted women voting rights. Four more introduced it on the same day as the federal vote and ten more by the end of 1972. The State of Appenzell held out for another 20 years. The women in my family had a lot to say about the event that evening. Women were looking forward to participating in our Swiss democracy at last.

1974 was nearly at its end when my family and I received a staggering blow. The unexpected death of my doctor on December 19th plunged us and the entire community into a state of profound grief. My interior was the scene of sadness and tears. Articles in all the newspapers reiterated the respect he received from his vast network of patients and how much he was esteemed and revered in our town. He was lauded for his talent and love of music, as well as his profound Christian faith. His brother-in-law, a Bishop, officiated his funeral services. His children and I would have to struggle on without him, comforted only by the knowledge that he had, at last, joined his beloved wife for eternity.

The death of my doctor was the end of an era for me. The years following this tragic event remain a blur in my memory. Everything was changing, including the neighborhood. My beloved Casino-theatre, built just 10 years before I arrived in the neighborhood, had become a cinema in 1945. Now in 1977, a casualty of television and a changing way of life, it was transformed into a Spanish community center, to the immense pleasure of the Spanish immigrants working at the canning factory. I noticed that many of the automobiles passing on Avenue de la Gare were Japanese models. Goods of all kinds were arriving from Asia, where American and European industrialists had gone to look for cheaper labor and higher profits, leaving empty factories and unemployment behind them in their own countries.

During this time, my rooms were occupied by members of the family or occasional renters. My cost and maintenance presented unsurmountable difficulties for the remaining members of the family. No one knew what to do with me. One evening there was a family conference in my *petit salon*, and I heard the unthinkable pronounced. It was decided that I would be sold. I was shocked and worried about my future. In the months that followed, furniture was moved around, possessions distributed, keepsakes sorted and divided among family members. Day after day, I became emptier and more abandoned.

As the sun set over the Jura plateau, the last member of my family pulled the front door shut, turned the key in the lock, and slipped it through the slot in my front door. It fell into a box on the inside of the door with a hollow thud that echoed through my empty hall.

PART TWO

~ 14 ~

An early ray of light penetrated the cloudy window of my cold, bare kitchen, as best it could. There was just enough light to see the calendar on the wall proclaiming the year 1981 below a faded picture of the Alps. Out of habit, I looked at it every day, but since no one was living in my interior, there was no one to change it. It could have been last year's calendar. Silence blanketed my rooms; no people, no pets, no radio, no television, no newspapers, no heat, and no music. My light fixtures were gone. Bare wires dangled from the ceilings.

The elegant ivory-colored silk that covered my living room walls was now a muddy grey, except for the rectangular squares where paintings had once hung. Pieces of plaster had fallen off the crown molding that contoured my ceilings, leaving gaps in the profile. My windows were milky and curtainless. I could hear mice in my attic and feel their furry bodies scurrying across the floor. A colony of bats had taken up residence in my entry hall. Their tiny claws clutched the ridges of the vault that formed the ceiling. I didn't mind them. They were welcome to stay. Except for the squirrel that jumped from the cedar tree onto my balcony, the bats and the mice were the only living things around me. It was sad to see my gravel alleys, once so precise and geometric, overgrown with grass. The little water basin in my back yard was clogged with dead leaves and sheep were eating the weeds around my tennis court.

A few people had come with the real estate agent trying valiantly to find me a new owner. I saw a scowling, fur-clad woman scrutinizing my rooms.

"Oh, no. This won't do at all. Look at the bathrooms! And the kitchen is so old-fashioned" she added, unnecessarily in my opinion.

"They could be renovated," the agent mumbled.

She took her passive husband by the arm.

"Come along, dear. We're wasting time here."

The agent raised his eyebrows and glanced at his colleague.

"Do we have any other inquiries?"

"Not for the moment. It's not going to be easy to find a buyer for this place in its present condition."

Summer had come and gone and the leaves on my chestnut tree turned their autumn-bronze color. A ground fog settled into the recesses of the shrubbery and the chilly air formed a mist on my windows.

"How old is the heating system?" a man in my petit salon asked.

"1970" the agent answered.

"Fuel oil prices are sky-high this year. It must cost a mint to heat this place."

That's what I hear all the time: too big, too expensive

to heat, run-down, old-fashioned, needs work, etc. etc. I hadn't seen anyone among the candidates that I wanted as an owner, not that I had a choice. I could see the real estate agents were getting discouraged and I doubted they would find a buyer before winter. The sun came up on another depressing day and the silence was becoming unbearable.

Attendez! Wait! ...something is happening.

The two familiar men from the agency were back in my living room. From their gestures, I could see they were excited. They had received an offer from someone who wanted to buy me.

"They're foreigners," one of them said. "That complicates everything. They say they have a residence permit, but I'll talk to them about it again. I don't want to turn up at the notary office and have legal complications block the sale. They're not European, you know."

I learned that the sale was notarized by none other than my boy, Henry, who was only four years old when he moved into my interior in 1912. He was nearly 80 now and had long since retired, but it was the family's desire that he notarize the changeover to the new owner. Maître Henry used a manual typewriter. The contract was typed with three carbon copies and the changes had to be kept to a strict minimum to avoid having to retype the whole thing. I was sold 'telle quelle', that is to say in the condition I was found at the time of the sale, no guarantees. Not terribly flattering for me.

The foreigners came only on the weekends in the beginning and did everything they could think of to chase the bats out of my hallway. They didn't succeed. In the end, they closed off the entry hall, opened the front door, and went home for the week. There was nothing to steal in my interior. The bats finally gave up the squat and found lodging elsewhere.

It was getting cold and I was keen on having my new owners move in and turn on the heat. I was looking forward to hearing conversations in my interior again and having my Journal delivered so I could catch up on all the news and activities of our local societies. I must have missed a lot during the time I was uninhabited.

At last, the day came that my new owners stood in my entry hall. The family consisted of a tall, solid-looking middle-aged man, a younger wife, a delightful little red-haired boy I hadn't seen before, a German shepherd called Nitro and a Siamese cat named Glycerin. I was anxious to hear what impression I made on the family and what they had to say about me.

Mon Dieu! Something is wrong! Terribly, terribly wrong!

I can't understand a word they are saying. They're speaking some kind of gibberish that makes no sense at all. When I heard they weren't European, I hadn't thought of the risk they might not speak French. How were they going to communicate with the tradesmen and the neighbors? After remaining empty and silent for so long, it was a terrible setback. I wondered what other unpleasant surprises were in store for me. It wasn't long before a neighbor showed up and I discovered that my foreigners spoke French as well as gibberish. I was a bit put out that they didn't speak French all the time for my benefit. I was trying hard not to form a negative attitude toward them.

Worse was yet to come! They changed my name. Can you imagine? I didn't think such a thing was possible or even legal. For seven decades, I had been known as The Villa St. Pierre. What was the neighborhood going to think?

The husband had fallen in love with me at first sight, which I deemed to be understandable. His wife's dream house, however, was a modern chalet with lots of windows overlooking Lake Leman. She was heartbroken that her husband wanted me instead. Even if we didn't hit it off right away, I had to admire her. It's not every woman who will give her husband up to another to ensure his happiness.

"You're just like Lady Baltimore," the husband said.

"I am going to rename this house My Lady's Manor."

"Lady Baltimore! Who's she?"

"She was the wife of Lord Baltimore, governor of the colony of Maryland under King George, three hundred years ago. Lord Baltimore gave her 10,000 acres of land on the Atlantic coast and built a manor on it to persuade her to live in the colony. He named the estate My Lady's Manor. I grew up on that land. It has been subdivided many times over the last two centuries. The countryside around here reminds me of Maryland, with lots of tobacco growers and horses. Well, that's the story, my lady," he said folding her tenderly in his arms. I was compelled to forgive him because what he did was out of love for me, and perhaps, a little lack of knowledge. From an architectural standpoint, I am a *Maison de maître*, a town mansion and not a manor, which is found in the countryside.

My foreigners set to work immediately replacing my drainpipes and other repairs that were critical before the onset of winter. It was urgent to understand the heating system. An inspection revealed an empty cistern.

"We'll have to order fuel oil," the husband said. "I wonder who we should buy it from?"

"Our neighbor, Monsieur Chanez, sells fuel oil. He might be willing to show us how the system works if we buy oil from him," his wife reasoned.

"Ok, I'll invite him over."

Monsieur Chanez came and after a friendly chat and a glass of white wine in my petit salon, they all went down to the furnace room in my basement. When the couple felt they understood the system sufficiently, they asked,

"Can you fill the cistern, Monsieur Chanez? Do you know how many liters it holds?"

"9000 liters, but you don't need to buy fuel oil." M. Chanez answered.

"Why on earth not?"

"Well, there's another cistern the same size underground and it's full. I know, because I filled it." M. Chanez said with a smile.

So, I had suffered all last winter with no heat while sitting on 9000 liters of fuel oil. Well, it was a nice bonus for my foreigners who had had the courage to buy me 'telle quelle'.

The faded calendar in my kitchen was dumped in the bin, a symbol of the refreshing change in my existence.

Newspapers and magazines appeared around the house again, but now they were called the International Herald Tribune, Time, Newsweek, and National Geographic and I couldn't read them. While my new family worked on my interior, they played western music: Kenny Rogers, Jim Reeves, and Patsy Cline. I was accustomed to Mozart, Beethoven, and Brahms and I had never heard music like that before.

The radio was hardly ever turned off, so after my long period of silence, I was able to catch up on what was happening in the outside world again. Our city band, La Perseverance, was celebrating its 100th birthday. The Fribourg radio station aired several of their best-known performances. A retrospective concert would be organized in March. It felt wonderful to be informed again. A few weeks later, I was delighted to find a copy of La Liberté in my letterbox. My foreigners spread it out on the dining room table just like Madame had done in the past. It was reassuring to return to an old habit of reading by the light of the bay window.

The Journal described an audacious project in town that had transpired while I was uninhabited and I knew nothing about it. It was the birth of a shopping center that promised to revitalize the local economy. Instead of being a modern complex outside town, as shopping centers usually were, this was the entire Rue du Camus on the north side of the old town. Starting on the corner with farm buildings belonging to the Dominican sisters, the street was currently undergoing a complete transformation to accommodate a pharmacy, butcher shop, grocery store, and a music store at street level. The realization of this shopping complex was no small matter due to the constraints of building in our ancient town. The population embraced this intelligent initiative that would slow the exodus of local customers to large shopping centers in the region.

Years later, when a frenzy of construction, development, and transformation took place, it was feared that our old town center would not be adequately preserved. To prevent foreseeable damage to our heritage by voracious promoters, a group of residents created an association for the Defense of the Old Town. Thanks to the de Vevey family, one of the oldest in our town, the association was able to prepare a catalog of images of the buildings inside the ramparts. The association clarified that their aim was to collaborate in the harmonious development of a lively energetic city that preserved its medieval appearance and its unique character.

While I was isolated from the outside world, a dispute about water treatment and sidewalks was going on between the town and its largest industry, the canning and milk processing factory. In the mid-1950s, when the first buildings of the canning factory appeared outside the ancient walls of the town, no one imagined the massive size of the factory a few decades later. With a yearly turnover of 240 million francs, it had become a giant looming at the city gate. The ever-expanding footprint of the factory, a stone's throw from the ramparts, left no one indifferent. Although heated discussions occasionally took place between the industry, who employed one-quarter of the working population of the town and the authorities, they were usually resolved. It was in the best interests of everyone to cooperate.

I was still quite a novelty among the friends of my new owners and visitors dropped in frequently to have a look at me. Some friends on their way to Bern asked,

"What made you choose this behemoth, Jack? You're a family of three."

"Old world charm and the layout. I need office space. The annex is perfect. "

"Couldn't you have found something more modern?"

"Of course," replied Jack. But who wants to live in a soulless, modern bunker when you can have a house with character and history of its own? Besides, we're good at fixing things up."

I decided I was going to like Jack.

For several years, I had felt a serious erosion on the corner pillar of my portico and was afraid of irreparable damage. I was relieved when my new owners disassembled the portico and replaced the deteriorating parts. Along Avenue de la Gare, people stopped again to see what was going on and speculated on who my new occupants were. It was like 1911 when I was being built and the horse-drawn carriages of the curious stopped in front of my gate. Only now, people were driving cars and if one stopped, the cars behind honked their horns impatiently.

My new occupants worked long hours and throughout the weekends. Being foreigners, they didn't know they weren't supposed to work on Sunday, a day of worship and rest in this devoutly Catholic area. Upon being reminded of the local customs by the neighbors, they transferred their renovation activities to my interior on Sundays.

One night, shortly after my new owners moved in, my interior from the attic to the basement was filled with soldiers. It reminded me of 1914, when 3000 infantry soldiers marched into town and stayed overnight. That had been my first experience as a garrison. Jack was working late as he was in the habit of doing when there was a knock on my front door. A Swiss Army Captain stood on my doorstep.

"Sorry to disturb you," he said. "We're doing maneuvers in the area and I need a place for my men to sleep. We planned to use the school across the street, but it's closed and we haven't been able to find the caretaker. I saw a light on here and wondered if some of my men could spend the night in your house?"

"Of course, come in. We've just moved in and the house is a mess but there's plenty of room. How many men do you have?"

"About a dozen," the captain said.

My owner took the officer to my unused second floor and attic and then down to the basement and the annex. He stationed a guard next to the front door and one in the hall below the stairs.

Following hand signals, the soldiers filed into the house, down the hall, and up the stairs. A dozen men passed, then twenty, thirty, forty, fifty, sixty...

Jack approached the captain.

"Just how many men do you really have, Sir?"

"Just how many men do you really have, Sir?"

"101. We've been joined by some other groups. It looked like there was enough room here."

My well-guarded front door.

"Swiss Defence 101," murmured Jack. But I don't know what he meant by that.

The next morning, the sun rose on the strangest sight. There were soldiers sleeping in my living room, petit salon, and the upper floors, where they had arrived during the night without making a sound. A field kitchen had been set up in the basement of my annex where breakfast was being prepared for the troop.

Placing a cup of coffee a safe distance away from the bed, Jack gently woke his wife.

"Now don't panic, Phyllie. A hundred soldiers moved into the house overnight."

"What?" she cried, jerking up to a sitting position.

"Whose soldiers? Have we been invaded?"

"Drink your coffee and I'll tell you all about it."

She listened to the incredible events of the night. A female acquaintance had arrived the day before and was sleeping in the guest room. In the excitement, the couple had completely forgotten about her.

"You better explain the situation to her, so she doesn't walk into the living room in her underwear."

"Right. This is going to be fun."

The guest, a 40-year-old divorced American woman, was delighted with the turn of events.

"A hundred soldiers! Wow! You really know how to entertain a girl."

During the week that the army bivouacked in my interior, the guest played the piano in the evening. When she left for the States, she was heard saying, "When I was in Europe entertaining the troops..."

Jeeps arrived with supplies and meals were prepared in the canteen in the basement. The little boy and his friends were delighted with the chocolate rations the soldiers gave them. Rifles were stacked in the garden in tipis and Nitro our German Shepperd, proudly patrolled the perimeter with an officer. When Friday came, the soldiers disappeared as suddenly as they had arrived. It had been an exciting week and when the army was gone, my rooms felt incredibly empty. My family picked up their routine, acutely aware of a vast amount of space around them.

~ 15 ~

Piles of wood accumulated along my perimeter as the clearing of my garden continued. Trees that had receded in total anarchy were cut down and low-hanging branches on the remaining ones were pruned. A pleasant smoky smell of burning wood wafted around me every weekend. There was a bit of trouble over the seeding of the grass. Flocks of birds landed in my garden to sample the excellent grass seed provided by my new owners. The seed was gone in a minute.

"Where did all these birds come from?" Phyllie asked the neighbor.

"From the Grande Cariçaie!"

"And what's that?"

"A nature reserve down by the lake, home to tens of thousands of migrating and indigenous birds," was the answer.

The grass was reseeded for the third time and pinwheels stuck in the ground to ward off the birds. My owners were bound to hear more about the Grande Cariçaie. There had been passionate conflicts, contradictions, and bitter litigation over the use of this land. Its 3000 hectares were colonized by a multitude of species of birds and animals. A nature reserve was created to protect them under the jurisdiction of the Association de la Grande Cariçaie. Some of the migrating species were so happy there, they settled down and migrated no more.

Christmas came and a huge floor-to-ceiling tree was installed in my petit salon, the Christmas lights connected directly into the wires where the ceiling light had been removed. I was amused to see the tree had become the favorite perch of Glycerin, the Siamese cat. As the year came to an end, I was feeling much better about my foreigners.

A calendar for 1983 appeared on my kitchen wall. It had been brought home by Phyllie.

"I bought a Swatch," she said, "and they gave me a calendar."

"What on earth is a Swatch?"

"It means 'second watch'. It's a new low-cost, high-tech Swiss watch. Very fashionable, all kinds of colors."

"Do you think there's a market for cheap Swiss watches?" her husband asked.

"I don't know. We'll see. Not everyone wants to wear the same watch all their life."

She was right. Amid extensive publicity, the Swatch watch was launched with articles and publicity in all the newspapers. The watch industry was in a severe crisis. Foreign competition, particularly Japanese, with its mass production of cheap electronic products, had established a foothold in the watch market. Under the direction of Nicolas Hayek in Neuchâtel, The Swatch Group achieved worldwide renown and played a key role in the revival of the watchmaking industry. Symbolizing its spectacular success, twenty years later it acquired the luxury jewelry company, Harry Winston of New York, for 711 million Swiss Francs. To celebrate, they bought the world's biggest flawless blue diamond, The Winston Blue.

I was well informed on the subject of watchmaking because of books I had seen at the time of my first owners. The Swiss watch industry owed a lot to Calvin, the Protestant reformer in Geneva who died in 1564. Under his strict rule, any display of wealth or wearing of jewelry was banned. Watches were not considered jewelry at the time. Geneva known for fine jewelry turned to watchmaking and soon became crowded with watchmakers. Seeking room to ply their trade, they spread out to the Jura and Lake Neuchâtel. In the 17th century, entire families in the State of Neuchâtel were employed in the watchmaking industry, chiefly making pocket watches and scientific instruments. Ninety percent of the Swiss watch production was concentrated in the arc of the Jura and around our lake. Tourist brochures call the region Watch Valley and trace an itinerary to the most famous watchmakers and museums. Phyllie's Swatch, as inexpensive as it was, was a good investment. The Swatch was here to stay.

As time passed, Jack was as devoted to me as ever and I was relieved to see that I had also won his wife's affection. Whereas I may not have been her dream house, I was a dream renovation project. Since I had so many rooms, supplies could be left wherever the work was being done. Time was never wasted putting paint and tools away and taking them out again. Brisk progress had been made in the renovation of my hallway but suddenly the work had come to a halt. Phyllie sat in my living room for hours grappling with some problem.

"I don't know what to do," she told Jack one afternoon. "These heavy velvet drapes are vestiges of another era and it feels like sacrilege to remove them. I admit that I'm intimidated by the women who chose them. She probably wouldn't approve of me taking them down. The problem is, the valences extend half a meter into the room. They're so dominating that I can't get the feel of the room."

"My dear," her husband said, "If the intimidating woman who chose those drapes walked into this room today, she would say, "

"Good Lord, are those old curtains still up?"

Phyllie laughed and I thought about Madame, my patron who had chosen those drapes. Jack was right. She would have thrown them out years ago.

Two days later, Jack helped her strip the room completely.

"I want to take everything off the walls and the windows," she said. "When the room is empty, it will tell me what it wants."

I was so pleased to hear her talk like that. It meant that she was paying attention to my personality and character. My living room project went on for more than a year. The delicately carved moldings around the silk wall panels were dismantled, numbered, and stored. When the trim came off, the original silk now stained and moldy was removed. To their delight, my owners discovered the signature of the original decorator G. Moser et H. Cottier, Tapissiers chez Les fils de Henri Bobaing and the date 1912, written on the plaster. It was the second time I had

My living room.

seen the inscription. Seventy years ago, I watched as the decorators wrote their names on the wall.

An interior decorator came to install new cloth in the panels. He looked at the signature on the plaster, thought for a moment, pulled out a pencil and wrote his own name below it and the date. Then getting to work, he installed a thermal aluminum-faced layer of insulation on the walls and overlaid it with an ivory cloth that had a diamond-shaped pattern like the original. The moldings were re-attached and repainted gold and ivory with a fine brush. The heavy drapery was replaced by sheer curtains in a matching color. I was pleased with the effect. My elegant living room felt light and airy.

In February, the committee for the organization of the Mardi-Gras decided to assemble its parade on Route de St. Pierre.

Under the guardianship of the statue of St. Pierre, this quiet obscure little street turned from its peaceful existence to a colorful, exuberant din of cacophony. Tractor-based floats with musicians, dancers, and children maneuvered into place. Musicians tuned their instruments, children shouted and threw confetti, while Guggen groups practiced their discordant music. Members of the sports clubs stretched their tendons and ran in place. To my foreigners, it looked like total bedlam, however, they joined in the fun and passed out white wine to the participants and chocolate to the children.

"Did you go to see the hanging of the perch?" One of the neighbors asked Jack.

"Hanging of the perch? No, we didn't know about that. Why did you hang him? What did he do?"

"No, no, you don't understand." laughed the neighbor.

"We hang him on a pole, parade him through the streets, then we set him on fire."

"Best not to be a perch around here," whispered Phyllie.

Before further explanation could be had, a whistle blew and the neighbor joined his group. The floats, bands, and groups marched down the street toward town along with my foreigners who still had a lot to learn about the local folklore. The perch was an immense papermaché reproduction that was burned to symbolize the end of winter.

Under a thick layer of confetti, the little street returned to its serene existence under the amused gaze of the statue of St. Pierre.

The next event in the annual cycle of festivities would be Surrexit and then Easter. Spring was announced by the crocus and bright yellow *bouton d'or* in my garden and the cozy warm temperature of my façade. The trees blossomed around me and in the surrounding countryside. Jack celebrated his 55th birthday and Phyllie bought him, and me, two stone lions. They were mounted on pedestals on either side of the stairway at my main entrance. They reminded me of the photos I had seen of Paris in the Illustration magazine back in 1912. Everything was new to me then and I had been impressed with the statues I saw along the bridges over the Seine.

The comings and goings of my foreigners were closely observed by the neighborhood. They had settled in better than I had expected and made friends easily, but I wondered if they were going to be able to adjust to our local customs and way of life. The Saturday before Easter, a neighbor was in the house and said he would be singing in the Surrexit procession. The American couple was fascinated by this ancient custom and asked if they could participate.

"Are you Catholic?" the neighbor asked Jack.

"No."

"Can you sing?"

"No."

"I can sing," offered Phyllie.

"Sorry, it's only for men," said the neighbor.

"Oh! Well, maybe we could just follow the procession."

"You can do that. Lots of people do. It starts at midnight at the church. Wear warm clothes."

Midnight the Saturday before Easter found my foreigners, bundled up and leaving the church struggling to keep up with the brisk march of the Surrexit singers.

As my renovation progressed, my 3.2-meter ceilings presented a lighting problem. The ceiling lights in my dining room and salons were bare bulbs hanging by their electrical cords and lit nothing but the ceiling itself. Phyllie and Jack suspended a wastepaper basket on a rope in my dining room and slowly lowered it until it was the right distance from the ceiling. It was amusing to watch them. The verdict was: one-meter-long chandeliers. The couple printed up decorator's business cards and went off to Milan in Italy to buy me light fixtures at a forty percent discount. In due course, three large crates arrived from Italy. When the chandeliers were installed, one each in my living room, petit salon, and dining room, I must say the effect was grand. Reflected in the mirror over my fireplace, it was a hall of mirrors like I had seen in the pictures of Versailles in my early *Illustration* magazines. Much smaller...of course.

Two black and gold statues holding up chandeliers were fitted on either side of my staircase. They were tall enough to light the entire hallway, which solved the problem of not having a ceiling light. The side panels in my living room needed sconces, so Jack drew a lovely three-branch motif, photographed it and sent it to Italy to be made. I thought about my Italian workers in 1912. They would have been proud of the way I looked with my new Italian furnishings.

Even the chicken coop that had been so useful during the years of rationing, became part of the renovation. It became a garden bar. The pigpen was transformed into a tool shed and a two-layer terrace was added all around it. Phyllie's brother came all the way from the United States to lay the stone. I was proud of that international touch. In the areas of my land that were still untamed, the little boy romped joyously with his school friends, hiding in the bushes and leaping over obstacles. Madame Ding, a cheerful, warm-hearted lady from a nearby village, came and took great care to keep my interior tidy. My parking lot was resplendent with a Maserati Indy and a Ferrari GT330, that Jack loved to drive over the Col de Cheyres. Nitro, the massive Alsatian, patrolled my limits and protected me from intruders while Glycerin kept rodents at bay. I had a real family again. My halls echoed with the footsteps of running children and my dining room rang with the laughter of guests and the clink of glasses.

One afternoon, Jack leaned against the doorway of my annex and said,

"I'll be leaving on Thursday. While I'm gone, have a look at what we can do with the furniture in here and order a telex from the PTT." The next morning, Phyllie wandered through my former medical office and looked at its walls lined with dull yellow metal cabinets. She noted the syringe filled with a brown liquid next to a used swab on the operating table, the bottles of cloudy liquid with lumps floating in them, the speckled wicked-looking forceps, and called the PTT about the telex. The rest could wait until the boss got back.

My telex was the first one in town. A very hi-tech system used for sending written messages converted into signals which were transmitted and printed out in another place. It rattled away and spat out long sheets of paper all by itself, even during the night. Jack traveled in the Middle East contracting with the sheiks for radar installations and complex communication systems while Phyllie managed the office. The Middle East working schedule, Saturday afternoon to Thursday, made a home office a practical solution.

Phyllie and me

It allowed Phyllie more time for her son and for me. She worked continuously on my renovation while her husband was away. I was flattered by all this attention. Her family was in the building trade and she had learned woodworking and masonry skills while growing up. She bought professional building supplies and a ten-meter-high rolling scaffolding, on which she seemed completely at home. During this period, I got to know her well. We became very close, in fact, she was literally stuck to my façade, sanding, scraping, painting, and rust-proofing every centimeter. Fourteen different products were needed to complete the necessary operations on a 2.5-meter-wide vertical slice of my façade. Then she rolled the scaffolding to the next swath, secured it and repeated the process. I don't know if it is normal for a woman to do this kind of work, none I had ever known did, but I have no idea what women do in America.

A parade of interesting and exotic visitors came and went in my interior. I was enjoying this satisfying diversion. Businessmen from India brought their wives with them. The ladies wore lovely flowing silk saris in bright colors. My owners liked to cook and often entertained their guests and clients in my rooms. The visitors from India presented a challenge if they were Brahman, strict vegetarians. When they came, my owners relied on Swiss standbys like Cheese Fondue and Raclette. If they were lucky, it was asparagus season.

Guests also came from Jordan, Morocco, Kuwait, Abu Dhabi, Greece, and Turkey. Sometimes the Arab men wore their dishdashis and ghutras but usually when they were in Europe, they wore suits and ties. There were often Arab men in my rooms in the summer. One of our frequent guests, Mohamed from Jordan called and said,

"Hello, Jack. It's getting hot over here. I think I'll come to discuss business with you in Switzerland."

"Happens to be Ramadan as well, isn't it, Moh?"

The holy month of Ramadan imposed rigid restrictions on Islamic believers. Mohamed was not particularly devout and found Ramadan a good time to be back in Europe where he had been educated.

Having heard that Bénichon was a harvest festival, Phyllie and Jack invited the neighbors and served them a Turkey dinner. The surprised guests explained the special menu normally eaten for Bénichon and the Americans described the Thanksgiving holiday. Although local tradition was distorted somewhat that year, the neighbors enjoyed the meal and had a new topic of conversation.

I mentioned that my foreigners liked to cook. Besides European food, they also made things like tacos, fajitas, tortillas, and enchiladas. My kitchen smelled of hot peppers, cardamom, and cilantro. They invited Swiss friends for dinner and said,

"You might find this food a little spicy. It's from California, near the Mexican border, where we used to live."

Observing the watering eyes of the guests, I feared they may have overestimated the Swiss tolerance for jalapeno peppers.

As time went on, the telex machine in my annex was replaced by a fax machine. The fax allowed both pictures and text to be transmitted. I missed my telex machine. I had become accustomed to the wood-sawing sound it made as it raced across the page, especially during the night when there were no other sounds in my interior.

The Sunday closest to August 10th arrived and the celebration of one of our oldest traditions; the blessing of the boats. I had read articles about it in the newspapers off and on for over a century. It was a very important day for our Noble Brotherhood of Fishermen. The event started with Mass at the church and a procession down to the port where the boats and fishing gear were blessed. The brothers come mostly from fishing families and maintain fraternal bonds of solidarity and mutual aid. At official ceremonies such as this, they are recognized by their dress: jerseys with a wave insignia, dark pants and shoes, beret and scarf. The color of the wave insignia on the jersey varies according to a prescribed hierarchy: fellow fishermen, fellow companions, fellow chaplains, honorary colleagues. To be admitted to the Noble Brotherhood of Fishermen, applicants must be sponsored by a member and accepted by two-thirds of the assembly of brothers.

Phyllie and Jack, always interested in the local folklore, followed the procession from the collegial church to the port along with the population of our town. On the way, back they passed in front of a ship chandler who had a little green sloop for sale in its yard. Its name was La Grenouille (the frog). That day, my family joined the ranks of the local boating population. They became members of the CVE sailing club and enrolled their young son in its weekly sailing lessons. At that blissful time, Phyllie was unaware of the solace and comfort La Grenouille would bring her in the difficult period that lay in her future. The following year, along with the other boats in the harbor,

La Grenouille was duly blessed on the Sunday closest to August 10th.

The squirrels in my cedar tree were already gathering nuts for the winter and my hydrangeas were starting to turn their autumn crimson color. I was enjoying the last days of summer, watching Jimmy, the little boy, playing with Nitro in the garden when my neighbor Monsieur Pillonel stopped by. He talked again about his mill. Up until 1950, it ran on waterpower and was equipped with a milling machine. A recent change in the law, abolishing federal aid to wheat producers forced his mill to close down along with 300 other mills. I was sorry to hear this news. Despite this setback, Monsieur Pillonel said he would continue to maintain the mill for its historic value.

Along with the autumn leaves, comes the Morat-Fribourg foot race. The 1985 edition registered an all-time record of 16,338 participants. The papers were full of enthusiastic articles. My visitor in 1933, who had competed in the first race with 13 other runners, must be over 70 now. If he was still alive, I wondered what he thought of the evolution of the race.

~ 16 ~

Phyllie was sitting on my portico enjoying the late autumn sunshine and reading Le Republicain when two men approached my front door. They were Americans and brought greetings from a mutual friend in Texas. The men were archaeologists. They were working on a project for the Earthwatch Foundation in coordination with the Neuchâtel Archeological Service to map the bottom of Lake Neuchâtel and identify Neolithic and Bronze Age artifacts. One of them was the eminent Dr. Ervan Garrison, professor, author, and pioneer in the technology of ground-looking radar. The archaeologists needed geographical coordinates to set up transponders along the lake that would provide them with the data they needed to map the bottom of the lake. They had been referred to Jack.

It was a pleasant opportunity for my family to be with other Americans. They spent the evening grilling steaks, laughing and criticizing United States foreign policy. The researchers came back again the next day when they discovered their instruments operating on 110 volts didn't work. They borrowed 220V equipment from the workshop and installed an antenna mast in the skylight of my attic.

Antennas were installed in two other locations on Lake Neuchâtel to complete the triangulation. It felt strange having this antenna mast sticking out of my roof night and day, but the birds seemed to like it. The archaeologists had worked on excavations all over the world and it was fascinating to listen to their conversations late into the night.

It was during this period, I learned that Lake Neuchâtel was part of one of the earliest inhabited regions in Europe. As the glaciers of the Ice Age melted, they left a swampy area with three puddles of water that came to be known as Lake Neuchâtel, Lake Morat, and Lake Bienne. In the spring, this area was sometimes flooded to the extent that it became one big lake. The Neolithic and Bronze Ages produced the first farmers in the region, who lived in houses built on stilts sunk into the swampy soil. Remains of this 5000-year-old pile-dwelling civilization can be found all around the shores of the three lakes.

In modern history, as the population grew, the regular floods in this marshy area waterlogged crops and propagated malaria. It was an unhealthy environment for humans and the population began to abandon their villages. The authorities in the region of the three lakes were forced to take action to combat the floods. Between 1868 and 1891, the largest river management intervention ever carried out in Switzerland was undertaken. This mammoth hydrological development program was referred to as "the correction of the waters of the Jura." Millions of cubic tons of earth were extracted to create the canals of the Thielle, Broye, Hagneck, and Nidau-Büren. With these four canals and various control dams, the level of the lakes of Morat, Neuchâtel, and Bienne dropped by 2.5 meters and formed a single communicating reservoir.

My interior was accumulating an extensive library of documents related to the correction of the waters of the Jura. As a result of the "correction," Lake Neuchâtel lost 23.7 km2 of its surface in the operation. Ports, wharves, and steamboats had to adapt to the new water level. The intervention was a success. The precious flat, dry land that emerged between the three lakes became a vast agricultural area; the vegetable garden of Switzerland. A new port control dam, completed in 1939, controlled the level of the three lakes and the flow of the Aare river. A regulation called the Murgenthal condition set the optimum flow of water. After a few decades, the drained area had subsided to the extent that a second correction was necessary. It was done between 1962 and 1973.

The lowering of the level of the three lakes brought to light an invaluable record of the lives of prehistoric humans submerged on the floors of lakes and riverbeds. Objects discovered included the oldest textiles in Europe, gold, amber, earthenware pots, dugouts and wooden wheels covered by water and silt. These harsh conditions hid them for many centuries from human scrutiny, but also preserved the artifacts virtually intact. Clusters of pylons formerly underwater were now sticking out of the mud all around the lake. The abundance of artifacts miraculously appearing on the newly exposed shores prompted a number of surveys and explorations at the time. The wooden pylons themselves were a mine of information about the lives of Europe's early agricultural communities. Dendrochronology, a method that dates wood with incredible precision, made it possible to trace the history of entire lakeside villages and the movement of their populations.

In the '80s and '90s, the projected motorway system funded by the federal government triggered an intensive period of archeological research in the three-lake region. With the sound of heavy road equipment revving in the background, a frantic effort was being made to save the physical record of the pile-dwelling settlements. It was for this reason that Dr. Garrison was sitting at my dining room table in the midst of instruments, charts and cables, drinking a beer. The Archaeological Service and the University of Neuchâtel spearheaded the project which included a team for underwater research. At the height of the research, nearly 200 archaeologists, technicians, and students from various countries were sifting through the mud of Lake Neuchâtel.

When the mapping was finished, Dr. Garrison and two other professors brought an Earthwatch team who would be diving on the sites marked as having potentially interesting artifacts. I didn't expect to see them back in my interior until their project was completed. Two days later, he reappeared on my doorstep looking troubled.

"What's the matter, Erv?" Jack asked. "You look down in the dumps."

Over a glass of wine in the office, the story came out. "It's the divers who have just arrived." I knew they wouldn't be professional divers, but I had hoped for a higher level. Diving conditions in this lake are far from the Caribbean sport diving these people have done. Visibility is low, there are thermoclines, and a lot of the work is in shallow water. Your friend in Texas told me you and your wife were divers. Any chance you could help us out?"

"I wish I could, but I am leaving for Egypt tomorrow," Jack said. Phyllie could do it if we can organize the office and family affairs. See what she says."

I didn't like the sound of this. I didn't think that it was healthy for my owner to be underwater and certainly not ladylike. Myself, I couldn't imagine why anyone would want to hang around on the bottom of a lake. A great effort had been made during my construction to ensure that I was waterproof. If I were underwater, my paint would come off, I would become moldy, my metal would rust and my wood would rot. I shudder to think of it. I listened with apprehension to the conversation between Phyllie and the professor.

"It's nice of you to ask me, but I don't know if I am qualified to do this kind of work."

You'll do just fine," said the professor patting her on the shoulder. "Shall we have a look at your gear?"

And that was that. The household was organized in such a manner that if the father was in the Middle East, a student came after school to help the little boy with his homework and stayed until his mother returned from the other end of the lake. During that period, I had com-pressed air tanks in my basement, rubbery uniforms and fins dripping from the clotheslines in my laundry room and bathing suits drying on my railings. There was a lot of excitement throughout the house over waterlogged pylons, old bones and pieces of perfectly useless broken pottery. The strange ways of humans never fail to astonish me.

I did, however, understand that this research led to a better understanding of the life that had inhabited the shores of Lake Neuchâtel throughout the Paleolithic, Neolithic, Bronze, Iron, and Roman ages. I heard Dr. Garrison, now a frequent guest in my interior, and Phyllie discussing a recent development. A new Metalor foundry was going to be built in Marin in the archaeologically rich area of La Tène. Metalor had long been a significant player in the Swiss economy and I remembered reading about its importance before and during the wars. Artifacts uncovered before the construction of the new facility showed that gold was already processed on this site during the Iron Age, more than 2,000 years before. The new site was named Latenor, reflecting the importance of its heritage.

In the same period of time, a spectacular discovery was made in the nearby town of Vallon. A Roman mosaic had been discovered and a meter or so uncovered. Vallon was on the road to the port of St. Blaise where the research raft was located and Dr. Garrison and Phyllie occasionally stopped on the way to work to see what was happening on the site. Meter by meter, the excavation progressed and the mosaic continued to unfold. There seemed to be no end to it. Excitement ran high in the archaeological community and the stop at Vallon became a daily routine. The result of the find was two mosaics of phenomenal dimensions and a wealth of artifacts where a prestigious

Roman villa had once stood. It had burned down, something I learned happened often to Roman villas because they were heated by a hypocaust, a system that channeled heat from a fire under the floor. The site eventually became the Roman Museum of Vallon.

For Phyllie, archaeological research was a seasonal occupation. Dr. Garrison himself and the underwater equipment generously donated by his university were only available during the summer. When fall came, the sub-bottom profiler, magnetometer, side-scan sonar and other instruments were carefully packed up and shipped back to the USA until the next season. My owners said goodbye to Dr. Garrison, who had become a close friend, and returned to their normal occupations. I would miss the charismatic archaeologist in my rooms and even the puddles of water and smell of neoprene and algae in my basement.

We were enjoying a period of prosperity in our region, a sharp contrast to the economic devastation we had experienced after the war. Captains of our regional industry like Nicolas Hayek and Guido Reuge demonstrated how determination and innovation could bring success. In St. Croix, the gamble of Guido Reuge to make music boxes in the face of all odds had paid off. He became the world leader in luxury music boxes. Our economy also received a boost from the Federal Government who implemented a visionary plan. It created a private research and development center CSEM (Centre Suisse d'Electronique et de Microtechnique). Neuchâtel, with its long tradition of watchmaking and microtechnology, proved to be the ideal location for this groundbreaking center of innovation.

CSEM supplied technological solutions to a broad range of markets, including automotive, medical, machine tools, and space exploration, and provided high-tech jobs for the young people of the region. The future of the economy on the north end of the lake was looking good.

By 1987, my new family had occupied my rooms for five years. They had done an amazing job of putting me back in shape. Jack worked for a firm outside Zurich, that hired him as a consultant for the Middle East. Once a year, his boss and all the employees of the firm were invited to come to 'the manor,' as they now referred to me, for a picnic. My former chicken coop/garden bar was resplendent with an international variety of food: guacamole and chips, canapés, foie gras, avocado shrimp, ramequins au fromage, dolmas, ham, and cold drinks.

One year, the invitation was for a barbeque, and to my horror and that of my owners, the Zurich people presented their hosts with a live piglet. I overheard Phyllie whisper urgently,

"What are we expected to do? Kill the pig and barbeque it? We can't do that."

"I don't know. Maybe it's a custom of some sort in this country. I'll try to get a clue from the guys," he said.

An explanation was not forthcoming. I tried to keep track of the piglet as it ran around my garden, but it was impossible. Nitro, the German shepherd proved to be a blessing. The piglet took a liking to him and followed him around the garden, which at least made the situation manageable. One only had to call the dog and you got the pig as well.

Nitro and the piglet.

The nebulous situation wasn't resolved when the Zurich colleagues left at the end of the day.

"What on earth are we going to do with this pig?" Jack asked.

"Let's try Monsieur Pillonel at the mill." Phyllie suggested. "He has farm animals over there."

Off they went to see Monsieur Pillonel and asked him if he would take the piglet. After the hilarious explanation of how the pig came into their possession, to the vast relief of Phyllie and Jack, Monsieur Pillonel took the pig and integrated it into his collection of livestock in the area. He explained that there is a hierarchy among pigs that prevents one from simply dropping a new pig into an existing sounder.

With some trepidation, the couple invited their colleagues from Zurich back again the following year. This time, they brought a flagpole and cemented it into the ground in my front yard and attached an enormous American flag. Now, I looked like the American Embassy. Perhaps, Jack should consider changing jobs.

Fall had come again. Sugar beets were still delivered to

the railway station, but now the wagons were pulled by enormous John Deere tractors. One tractor wheel alone was as tall as the horses that pulled the wagons when I was young. A new cycle was emerging and modifying my annual routine. In the spring, the Surrexit procession was of considerable interest to visitors in the house who followed the procession. Summer brought the annual picnic and colleagues from Zurich, an event I now dreaded, as well as the arrival of Dr. Garrison who kidnapped Phyllie and took her to the bottom of the lake. My foreigners abandoned Thanksgiving, celebrated Bénichon in town and for the Recrotzon, went to Payerne for Chinese food.

I should clarify a detail about my location. I am in the State of Fribourg, but just barely. My town is an enclave, an ancient geographical patch, which belongs to the State of Fribourg but is completely surrounded by the State of Vaud. To complicate the matter further, Fribourg is a Catholic state and Vaud, a Protestant one. When our stores and restaurants are closed for Catholic holidays, one only needs to travel nine kilometers to the town of Payerne, where everything is open and functioning. My foreigners quickly picked up on this geographic anomaly.

During these wonderful years, my days were filled with exciting projects, interesting people, and my kitchen with exotic cooking odors. I became more beautiful every day and my new family showed me off with pride. Wrapped in my warm blanket of contentment, I didn't see the storm clouds gathering once again on my horizon.

~ 17 ~

Jack came back from Kuwait and consulted a doctor. The doctor shook his head gravely, and a battery of tests was done at the hospital. Phyllie and I and the little boy worried and waited anxiously for news. The dreaded word cancer was pronounced, and our bright world immediately dimmed. An operation was performed in Bern. While Jack was hospitalized, Phyllie struggled to keep the office running and reassure the worried little boy. Happily, the operation was successful, and Jack made a rapid recovery.

We breathed a collective sigh of relief and picked up our life where we had left off. Phyllie was optimistic, but I had already experienced the loss of Madame, my patron, and both my doctor and his wife. My long perspective endowed me with a more fatalistic outlook. For almost a year, everything was back to normal. Then the stress of Jack's job and the turmoil in the Middle East took their toll. A relapse deteriorated his health, and Phyllie began to make frequent trips to the Inselspital in Bern. Our vocabulary took on the words carcinoma, chemotherapy, IRM, and general metastasis. As time passed, our beloved Jack was unable to travel and soon unable to work at all.

He missed driving most of all and spent hours just sitting in his Ferrari in the parking lot, reliving better times. Finally, he was confined to a wheelchair. It was then that I discovered I was not suitably equipped for someone in a wheelchair. It had never occurred to me that the five steps at my front entrance would prove to be an obstacle. A local doctor and good friend had the necessary medical equipment installed in my interior so Jack could stay at home and spend his remaining weeks here with me in the place he loved most.

It was in my petit salon that he slipped away from us. He was buried in our cemetery, and when Easter came, the Surrexit procession stopped at his grave, it being the tomb of the last bourgeois buried in 1988. Phyllie was devastated. I had lived much longer than she and knew that grief was the price you paid for love. She was learning that now. Caring for her son was her only consolation, and I was beginning to fret about my own future. Renovation of my rooms and maintenance on my structure had once again come to a halt. The family finances were depleted, and the family was left without an income. Silence and sadness replaced the sound of tools and laughter in our dark world.

The grief of my new widow was echoed in the world around us as a period of disasters came to a close. Every morning at seven, the radio came on, and I listened to the news. The commentator covered the depressing subjects of mad cow disease in the UK and the US bombing of Libya. Then, the Chernobyl Nuclear Power Station in Ukraine exploded, releasing radioactive material across much of

Europe, creating the worst nuclear accident in history. After a history of male domination, Elisabeth Kopp, the first woman Federal Council member in our government, resigned.

With the death of Jack, my small family was now even smaller. An enormous contrast from the days when my interior was filled with the doctor's six children. I felt cavernous and empty. I worried for the second time in my existence how a widow with a young boy was going to manage the maintenance and cost of my upkeep. To bring some life into my interior and to console her son, Phyllie bought a new German shepherd to replace Nitro, who, along with Glycerin, died in the calamitous year of 1988.

Commercial problems bubbled quickly to the surface. There were contracts in the Middle East that couldn't be completed and equipment ordered that was no longer deliverable. My new widow had none of the technical qualifications needed to deal with projects in progress in the Middle East, and it was out of the question that a woman alone would be granted a visa or be admitted into the Arab countries. Phyllie came from a family of independent entrepreneurs and immediately set about reorganizing Jack's corporate structure, working long hours to bring in funds. An internet modem and laptop computer appeared in my annex. Email replaced my fax, which had replaced my telex, which had replaced postal service.

Phyllie's faithful friend, Rosmarie, often stopped by to see how we were coping.

"Since Jack was a consultant, I guess his income will stop now," she said.

"It already has. His firm kept him on salary the whole time he was ill, which was very generous of them."

"The mortgage on the house is pretty heavy, I guess," Rosmarie observed.

"Yes. The rates have just gone up again. Highest they've ever been. I'll think of something. The equipment we sold in the Middle East will need spare parts. I can handle that."

"Could you transform the house? Convert the floors into separate apartments, for example?" Rosmarie asked.

I would love to, but the house won't let me. It would mean shutting off the stairwell and the window that brings light into the hall. And even then, the second floor could only be accessed by going through the apartment below it.

This house was built for a big family, and it's not going to submit to any other function.

I was pleased that Phyllie understood my architecture so well and wouldn't be wasting time trying to modify me.

"Well," Rosmarie said. "I'm sure you will make it. But if you need help, please tell me."

I was reassured that my new widow had a good friend she could count on. Their regular discussions kept me informed of the financial problems we were facing. My renovation had stopped, and I was worried about the maintenance of my structure.

I hoped that nothing major would go wrong with me that would require expensive repairs. I worried about the parts of my plumbing, heating, and electricity that had not yet been renovated.

It had been six months since Jack's funeral, and I could see that Phyllie was wearing down. She lost weight and lost patience with her son. She sent him to a friend in Washington State to do a year of high school in the USA. When the problems became too oppressive, she escaped to the middle of the lake in La Grenouille, her little green sailboat, where no one could reach her. As the firm slowly started to show a profit again and the financial crisis eased, a new dilemma emerged. She received a registered letter, by now a foreboding drama in itself.

Changes were being made to the neighborhood, and she was invited to go to an information session at the town hall.

Feeling helpless and lost, Phyllie gazed at the plans the town council had posted on a billboard and the architect's model on the table. According to the plans, a new bus depot was going to be built across the street from me on the pasture where the herd of black and white cows grazed. The depot was a massive hangar, out of place in our neighborhood. Looking closer at the urban plan, she received a shock. I was labeled on the plans as the new museum.

Fighting down a wave of panic, Phyllie looked around to see if there was anyone she knew at the meeting. She saw Thérèse, who took on the chimera of a shining angel. Thérèse was the wife of the doctor who had arranged for her husband to spend his last days at home with me, but much more important at that moment; she was the mayor of the town. With a deep breath to compose herself, she said

"Thérèse! Hello, how are you?" The reply went unheard.

"I don't know anything about Swiss law," Phyllie stammered.

"Can... can they do that? Can they take my house and make it a museum without consulting me?"

Thérèse looked puzzled. "No, of course not. Your house isn't involved in this plan. That's just an architect's conception."

After further reassurances, Phyllie returned home exhausted to face the rest of her problems. From that time on, we had very different opinions of architects. I thought they were benevolent creators like Monsieur Devolz, and she thought they were dangerous maniacs.

The building permit for the hangar was issued, and the land across from me was dug up. The unique little building called the Glacière Cardinal, which once housed blocks of ice, was demolished without a thought for its historical value. From the roof of my annex, I could see the foundation being laid with reinforced concrete and conduits installed for water, sewage, and electricity. Neighborhood gossip reached us that someone had appealed the decision to attribute the building permit, a common but rarely successful procedure.

Suddenly, everything stopped. The bulldozers disappeared, and the workmen vanished. Silence descended on the construction site. By starting the construction before the appeal deadline expired, the bus company had made a monumental error. To everyone's surprise, the court upheld the appeal and orders were handed down to remove the construction in progress.

Corporate heads rolled. For many years to come, I would gaze across the street and ponder human folly and a very, very expensive parking lot.

After her husband died and her son went away, there was a change in my relationship with Phyllie. She talked to me directly for the first time. I imagine she needed to think through her problems by expressing them aloud, and soon it became a habit. These curious one-way conversations took place in the living room at the end of the day when no one else was in the house. It wouldn't do for people to see her talking to the walls. She sat in an armchair in front of my marble fireplace and stared at the ceiling as the sun disappeared behind the Jura plateau.

"I'm going to repaper the *petit salon*," she said. "I'll replace that blue patterned wallpaper with a nice neutral beige. It will harmonize better with the other rooms."

I couldn't comment, but I agreed. I never liked the wallpaper in my *petit salon*.

"I will also be looking into some projects to bring in some revenue," she said.

Sounded good to me.

Soon after that, the morning sun shone through my bay window onto the dining room table, where people were taking notes while a teacher lectured them in French. A workshop for Swiss German teachers had been organized to improve the French they taught to primary school children. The mandatory program was three weeks long and stretched over a three-year period. It was designed to promote understanding between our national language areas and improve the teachers' French skills. The teachers lived in the town with host families and were supposed to speak exclusively French during their stay. I noticed they spoke their Swiss German dialect when they were alone, but their secret was safe with me.

Phyllie and her colleague, Jacques Reinhard, took them to visit our monuments and archaeological sites and explained our local history in French. They visited the Late Bronze Age reconstruction at Gletterens, the Roman ruins at Avenches, our castle, church, and the Dominican convent. Many of the teachers were surprised to discover the charm of our French-speaking *Welschland* and embraced the program with enthusiasm. When the rotation of the teachers was complete, they returned to their Swiss German schools, and Phyllie used the interval to paint the woodwork in my petit salon to match the new wallpaper. I always enjoyed these intimate moments alone with her and felt pampered by the care she took to find and test exactly the right color for my wainscoting.

"You remember Professor Garrison who mapped the lake, don't you?" Phyllie asked that evening. She was sitting in her favorite chair next to the fireplace.

"Well, he wants to bring some people to work in the area next year. I won't be able to house them all. I think I will start renovating the second floor."

I may not have mentioned my second floor. There were five rooms up there but nearly no electricity, heat, or water. One of the rooms had an upturned solidified bucket of tar in the center of the floor. The tar had penetrated the wooden planks of the floor and was impossible to remove.

The room on the north side was overflowing with plastic garbage bags filled to the top and tied off. With a mug of hot coffee in hand and a comfortable chair, Phyllie sat down near the window and started opening the bags. She had planned to spend half an hour sorting out what could be discarded.

The first bags were filled with medical receipts and advertisements for pharmaceutical products left from the medical office. Other sacks contained unfinished embroidery, moth-eaten curtains, and neatly sewn cotton blackout shades from the last war. One of the sacks was full of correspondence. She pulled up another chair and put the envelopes aside.

There were some colored postcards from 1915 to 1917, showing soldiers in impeccable uniforms and even boy soldiers. The backs of the postcards were filled completely with the tiny, meticulous handwriting of a soldier in the French Foreign Legion during the First World War. He was a brave soldier facing death daily in the trenches on the front lines. He wrote with affection to the widow who had built me. His chances of surviving the war were very slim. Phyllie was spellbound by the correspondence and was still squinting to read the small script in the disappearing light as the sun went down over the Jura.

She set the last card down, it read:

1st July 1916 Battle of the Somme
I am writing this card to tell you that I received your parcel and wish to thank you. Don't send me anything for

the moment. When you get this card, I will be dead or wounded. May God bless you. A good handshake all around. Jean Ansermet

Stretching her cramped legs, Phyllie struggled to her feet, tears streaming down her cheeks. I, of course, knew all about the brave legionnaire. Madame, my patron, had waited anxiously for the postcards to arrive in the mail during that terrible war.

Postcard sent from the trenches of WWI by Jean Ansermet.

~ 18 ~

The renovation of my second floor got a boost from a recession that closed down building projects in 1990 and left many local men unemployed. A Spanish couple rang my doorbell.

The husband had been laid off from a local construction company where he had worked as a crane operator. The couple, who had adult children in Spain and Switzerland, was preparing to pack up and go back to Spain. They needed temporary lodging.

This was the beginning of a love story between Phyllie and the Spanish couple, Amelia and Miguel. I provided living space for the couple, and Miguel helped with my maintenance. Together with my owner, they attacked the renovation of my second floor. The garbage bags went to the dump. The upended tar bucket was still rooted to the wooden floor and wouldn't budge. It shook me up a bit when they dislodged it with a serious whack of a sledge-hammer. No amount of sanding would make the tar disappear, so the floor was covered with a Sisal carpet. It was a familiar sensation having my walls covered with wallpaper. A wide brush smoothed the creamy glue over the surface, and then the wallpaper was overlaid. I remembered it being done long ago when my dining room was papered.

The sturdy burgundy damask paper was still in good condition. The smell of glue, window putty, and varnish filled the air. The sound of ladders scraping along the floor and the feel of sanders vibrating against my wood reminded me of the wonderful days when Jack was alive. My second floor was being transformed from an attic to a useful living space.

The Spanish couple brought the sound of laughter and tools back into my interior. My second-floor hall and alcove walls had cracks in the plaster that were too fine to fill. So Phyllie and Miguel covered them with a layer of stucco. It was a Botox facelift of sorts, no more wrinkles. Carpeting soundproofed the hall floor and muffled the squeaking floorboards. Furniture was found at the Coup de Pouce secondhand store on the way down to the lake. The rooms were given colors rather than numbers, the blue room, the pink room, etc. The jolly, round Amelia cooked, inspected the finished work, and pointed out anything less than perfect. My first-floor kitchen smelled of paella, jamón ibérico and tortilla espanola. Soon the archaeologists had the rooms they needed, as well as a bathroom and heating.

Phyllie relished all this activity, and I was pleased to see that sad, empty look less frequently on her face. As the evening shadows lengthened and the sun set over the Jura, she sat in her armchair next to the fireplace. I waited to hear what she had to tell me.

"The second floor is renovated now, and there are ten bedrooms available for guests. Dr. Garrison's team will be comfortable there. When they leave, you are going to become a B&B," she said.

What's a B&B? I wondered.

"B&B means Bed and Breakfast. It's a private house where people stay overnight and have breakfast. It's a common practice in English-speaking countries but not widely known here."

If I have 10 bedrooms, I could be a hotel, I thought.

"It's like a hotel," she continued, "but hotels have a bathroom for each room. That kind of modification would be too destructive for you and too expensive. The manager of the Tourist Office is coming to look at the rooms. She will be sending us guests. I hope it's going to work."

I hoped so too. There was no guarantee, but the promotion generated by the tourist office was bringing a lot of visitors to our town, and there was a shortage of rooms. A license didn't exist for B&B's, so Phyllie and I were issued an operating license for a snack bar. The redundant office desks were converted into tables, and a breakfast buffet was set up in the bay window of my dining room. Bed linen and towels arrived from Arizona, where Phyllie's super-shopper sister-in-law had been commissioned to buy them. Whatever dishes and kitchen utensils were needed came from the Coup de Pouce secondhand shop. I watched anxiously as the manager of the tourist office arrived to inspect the newly available accommodations.

"Wonderful, fantastic!" she panted as she arrived breathless on my second floor.

"What's a B&B?"

Each time a potential guest called for a room, they asked the same thing. Because of the name My Lady's Manor that Jack had given me, my function was sometimes misunderstood. After hanging up on a gravelly voice asking about the dimensions of Miss Breakfast, Phyllie published brochures in French, English, and German clearly describing our offer. Tourists came from all over Switzerland and other European countries for their summer vacations and events in the area. They visited our museum, now known as the Frog Museum, our historical monuments, the Grande Cariçaie nature reserve, and Watch Valley. The tourist office was delighted, Phyllie was relieved, and I began to feel better about my role as the central character in this revolutionary project.

Apache, the second German shepherd, who took his guard duty seriously, proved to be an unforeseen problem. The transition from private-house to bed-and-breakfast was patiently explained to him.

"Strangers were now going to be let into the house to earn money to buy dog food (among other things)."

Apache's approach to economics was eating the middleman. The method of introducing him to the smells of the guests by way of their personal effects, rather than their more vulnerable flesh and blood persons, proved to be a successful one. After that, Apache made the rounds of the rooms in the morning when the beds were made, and the rest of the day, his guard duty was confined to the office.

The B&B adventure turned out to be fun. Tourists

exclaimed their admiration for me when they walked into my entry hall and elegant living rooms. Naturally, I was flattered by their comments. They sat in my garden or my *petit salon* and discussed a wide range of subjects: love affairs, in-laws, taxes, problem adolescents, and politics. I couldn't help overhearing their intriguing conversations. I was never bored.

At this time, the population of Switzerland was debating whether or not to join the European Union, and there were animated discussions every morning at the breakfast table. A Frenchman said, "If you don't join, you will be isolated." A Canadian said, "Don't join, it will isolate you from the rest of the world."

A Belgian lady said, "It's wonderful. There will be 14'000 new offices in Brussels." A young German asked, "Is the European Union in Germany?" As a B&B, I was becoming very well informed on social and political affairs.

The B&B was filled to capacity for the 700th anniversary of the Swiss Confederation in 1991.

Television covered celebrations all over the country. Because of our medieval town center, our town was chosen for a historical reenactment. The town itself became a stage and went back in time to the year of our Lord, 1403. Our ancient streets rang with the laughter and shouts of the population in their finest costumes from the middle ages and the echo of horses' hoofs on the cobblestones. The smell of tanners treating animal hides and the beeswax of candle makers filled the air. Blacksmiths worked the bellows of their forges, their rhythmic tapping on hot metal in tune with the lute makers tuning their instruments. A wild boar turned on a spit in the middle of the street. Phyllie, dressed in her blue and grey medieval gown and veiled headdress, left the house to participate as a volunteer in the festival. I could see the flags flying from the towers in town and hear music being played on bagpipes. Because the festival was on the evening news, I was able to see what was happening and I didn't feel left out.

Every August, the narrow streets of our town are filled with a bustling open-air antique market. Dealers with stands at the market stayed in my rooms and talked late into the night about unusual objects, prices, and trends. They were among the visitors who most appreciated my vintage style. The jazz festival, the rose festival, the open-air music festival, the medieval festival, the bicycle race, and numerous sailing regattas brought a varied and interesting palette of guests. I especially liked the cyclists. Some had bicycled from 50 to 80 kilometers and arrived tired and sweaty. After a shower, they were in good humor and went out to eat in town. Bicycles came in all sizes, some with parents pulling their children in little trailers behind their own bicycles. The bicycles were stored in my garage to keep them dry and safe. I can proudly say that during all those years, not one went missing.

That year, it was my good fortune that one of the guests came from Zermatt, where he had hiked the Chamois Trail. On his departure, he left us a calendar for 1993 with a picture of a chamois on it. So finally, I could see what a chamois looked like. It was a deer-like mountain goat with ebony back-curved horns and a brown and white striped face. It had taken me more than 60 years to get that information.

The year had gone by quickly, and a new 1994 calendar was already on my kitchen wall. It had spectacular pictures taken by the Hubble Telescope. Our Swiss astronaut, Claude Nicol-lier, was on the team that had repaired it in space. I was looking forward to another year full of B&B adventures. It was a stimulating experience, and I was becoming known throughout the land. Among the visitors, a tiny Asian lady arrived one day on my doorstep. A local pastor among Phyllie's acquaintances asked that we find a way to take this person in. She was being counseled by the pastor and needed a family place to stay. A hotel wasn't suitable. So, naturally, I was the perfect solution.

"Please come in," Phyllie said. "We're fully booked, but there is a small room for children that isn't occupied."

"That will be fine. My name is Madame Chung. I would like to stay a few days."

Madame Chung stayed a week and visited the pastor every day. She was absolutely delightful. She was employed at the Paris Opera, where she sang in the choir and taught music.

When she left, she said she would be retiring from the Opera in a few years and would like to conduct a Master Class for classical music in my interior. During my B&B years, I had heard many people say they wanted to organize this and that, but the projects rarely materialized. I didn't expect to hear from Madame Chung again.

By the time the Blessing of the Boats had taken place, we were nearly through the summer vacation period. The very day the school vacation ended in Zurich and Basel, our town and my rooms were deserted. At the store across the street, a sign announcing early closing hours was propped up by a box of German-language children's books on sale at half price. French replaced the Swiss German dialect heard everywhere during the vacation season. The Bénichon arrived, and by then, Phyllie and the staff were exhausted. Our intern packed up and left for her fall school term in Basel or Bern. The last sailing regatta, the Morat-Fribourg foot race, and the autumn colors in my garden marked the end of the season. The squirrel family living in my cedar tree was busy packing nuts into a hole. I loved to watch the furry red creatures run up and down the branches and hop onto my balcony railing.

A familiar controversy was back in the news. During the last century, fishermen's cabins and lakeside family vacation chalets had been constructed on land allotted by the state or the city. The chalets now found themselves in the Grande Cariçaie. The nature reserve association considered them an intrusion and wanted them demolished. Many of them third-generation chalet owners had already spent years of litigation and legal fees trying to save their buildings.

The Grande Cariçaie, if left unattended, would be colonized by vegetation and become dry land, like the rest of the drained three-lake district. To combat this natural evolution, a firm with a half-million-franc budget and an inventory of heavy equipment maintained the reserve. Yet, little tolerance had been shown for the unwelcome chalets, and it was unclear when, if ever, this conflict would be resolved.

The Journal mentioned that this contradiction was not the only one on Lake Neuchâtel. Air Force fighter pilots fired on fixed and moving targets in the lake where ultra-protected birds nested in the nature reserve. The Forel firing range had been in use since 1926. Authorizations were granted in 1928 to create a permanent air-to-ground (air-to-water) firing range in the lake. It is still in use today. A sign posted at the sailing club warns boat owners to avoid the area near Forel from January to May and October to December when military target practice was scheduled. The tons of nonexplosive ammunition accumulated on the lake bottom for nearly a hundred years resembles a scene out of an apocalyptic war movie.

The month of October 1994 is engraved forever in the collective memory of our district. Shortly before midnight on October 4th, in the village of Cheiry, a fire broke out. Firefighters who were called to the scene discovered an appalling massacre. Twenty-three bodies were pulled from the rubble. The victims, members of the Order of the Solar Temple, were found dressed in ceremonial robes in an underground chapel lined with mirrors. The bodies lay in a circle, feet together, heads outward, most with plastic bags tied over their heads. The victims had ingested sedatives and been shot in the head. A few hours later, in three chalets in Granges-sur-Salvan in Valais, another 25 bodies were found. Several of them were children grouped together.

The tragedy was discovered when officers rushed to the

site to fight a fire ignited by remote-control devices, one of which did not function. The aspiration of the sect was to transit through a collective suicide to the star Sirius. Press coverage was international. TV reporters arrived in Cheiry in vans from as far away as the United States. While deaths by firearms can technically be considered murder in the State of Fribourg, it was difficult to distinguish those who had consented from those who were murdered. Despite the confirmation that the two known founders of the sect, Luc Jouret, and Jo Di Mambro were among the dead at Salvan, another massacre took place a year later in France, bringing the total body count to 74.

Almost everyone in town knew someone connected to the victims of the massacres; an acquaintance in a gym class, a friend of a friend, a colleague from work, a cleaning lady. A pall of sadness and shock hovered over our district as we struggled to understand how this tragedy could have happened. Our next holiday was St. Nicholas, celebrated the Sunday before December 6th. I heard the church was packed full of worshippers coming together to try to erase this demonic tragedy from their hearts and minds.

~ 19 ~

As the last rays of sunshine disappeared over the Jura, Phyllie put a match to the wood in the fireplace to take the chill out of the living room. Another winter had descended on my garden and covered it with a fluffy layer of snow. The lions on either side of my front steps looked regal, with little pyramids of snow on the top of their heads. She sat in her favorite chair, and I waited to hear what she had to say.

"The archaeologists are coming back," she said.

I wasn't happy to hear this. I thought she was going underwater again.

"I won't be working underwater this time," she said. "Professor Garrison is bringing students from his university in the United States to study in Switzerland as part of their curriculum starting in 1998."

She explained that the University of Georgia in Atlanta was a very progressive one and encouraged its students to study abroad. They set aside a period of time to do this in May and called it a Maymester. As I understood it, I was going to be an extension of the University. Before the students arrived, they were sent brochures with nice pictures of my portico, garden, and rooms, along with data about our local historical sites. I tried to imagine people looking at my picture in a faraway country like the United States, and I wondered what they thought of me.

Although I didn't know it yet, this was the beginning of my cultural period encompassing history, art, music, and film.

From then on, when the cherry trees were in bloom in May, my interior was filled with young people chattering in English.

There were also quiet periods when the students studied in their rooms or my living room, and exams which they took very seriously. Paradoxically, to make this foray into ancient history, I had to be equipped with the latest in electronic technology. WIFI, a network of waves, was installed in the house so the students could connect their computers to their University in Atlanta. I couldn't see or feel the waves, but the students seemed to be using them, so I guess they were there somewhere inside me. Once again, I was at the forefront of technology and was one of the first buildings in the town to be equipped with WIFI.

To provide an overview of the period to be studied, each student was issued a day-to-day program which provided me with information on what they were doing when they were not in my interior. The program started out with a lecture at the Laténium, Switzerland's largest archaeological museum near Neuchâtel. It stands on the spot where the most significant artifacts were discovered during the years of research and displays 3000 fascinating objects illustrating the everyday lives of the first inhabitants of the lake district. I overheard the professor and Phyllie discussing the artifacts on display at the museum when they came back to my rooms. One of the displays was a series of bronze rings found by their team in the '80s. The rings had been strung on a now-disintegrated leather strap, perhaps worn around the neck and used for payment 5000 years ago.

A screen was set up in my *petit salon*, where lectures were given by the professor, visiting Swiss teachers, and archaeologists. Along with the students, I learned that our three-lake region is something of an archaeological mecca, with a staggering 17,000 years of uninterrupted occupation. The earliest known buildings in Switzerland, prehistoric houses built on pylons between 5000 and 500 BC, were initially thought to be located in the lake itself. However, when fire pits were found under the pylons, it was concluded that they were built on the marshy and often flooded shoreline, and the pylons served as foundations. Many years later, it was announced to the press that the collective six-country pile-dwelling civilization was registered as a UNESCO Heritage Site, with half of the dwellings located in Switzerland. Only a few kilometers away, in the village of Gletterens, some of these early buildings had been reconstructed on the site where they were discovered. They are long one-room structures with thatched roofs made of clay, straw, and dung. There is also a small grain storage built on stilts. Our students spent an entire day at Gletterens, learning how to make arrows with flint, light fires without matches, cook game, and use a sagaie, a prehistoric javelin thrown with the aid of a propulsor.

Bronze-age longhouses at Gletterens.

Day after day, the students sat in my petit salon and listened to their professor's lectures. And so did I. I learned that in 58 BC, the Helvetii, the original people of Switzerland, upon losing a fierce battle at Mont Vully, became part of the Roman Empire. The impressive fortifications of the oppidum of Mont Vully had been reconstructed and were a favorite excursion for students. Part of their program was a visit to the ruins of the Roman city of Aventicum, its 5.6-kilometer city wall, Roman baths, and massive amphitheater. When the students returned to my rooms, their animated chatter told me what they had seen. They said they sat on the steps of the amphitheater and ate their picnics above the hypogeum, a network of tunnels, animal pens, and trap doors designed for gladiators and animal combat. Two thousand years earlier, in most Roman Arenas, the stench of blood and death would have pervaded the hypogeum. Now it was a pleasant place to picnic and reflect on a by-gone area.

When the student program was finished for the year, the students packed up and left for Georgia.

Phyllie sat in the living room, enjoying the calm of the empty house. It would soon be time to gear up for the summer B&B season.

"It was interesting having the American students here, wasn't it? I enjoyed their company," she said.

I agreed.

"The manager of the tourist office is coming tomorrow morning. She says she has a new project she wants to discuss."

I knew the manager of the tourist office. Her name was Isabella. Her exuberance probably came from her mother, who was Italian. Her father was German and her husband Swiss, but I could see no evidence of the structured influence they should have exerted on her personality. She had 25 ideas every day, and all of them were excellent. The problem was that nobody could keep up with her. It was always two weeks later when Phyllie grasped the idea Isabella had been trying to put across. I wondered what project she had in mind this time.

Isabella pulled her red convertible into my driveway and jumped out dressed in one of her bright, exotic outfits. Phyllie was already sitting at the table in the dining room. Before a cup of coffee could be poured, Isabella said,

"You know the problem we have with our summer season ending abruptly when the Swiss Germans return to school.

Well, I want to extend the season next year, so I'm bringing a group of artists to town to paint the medieval buildings and the castle in September. Paintings travel widely and are displayed in homes and public buildings for years. Through paintings, our town will become better known and attract more visitors.

The event will last for 10 days every year, and we will call it the September Pictorial. It will end with a painting contest for the public, children included, and we'll ask the businesses in town to prize money."

"How will you finance it?" Asked my ever-practical Phyllie when Isabella paused to take a breath.

"Each artist will donate one painting," she explained, "and we'll sell the paintings to pay their expenses while they're here.

This year the artists will come from Paris. I have already contacted an association of artists, and next year they will come from Bologna, then Prague, etc. We'll house them here."

"Here, at my place?" stuttered Phyllie. "How many of them will there be?"

"Oh, about a dozen, I imagine."

The artists came from Paris for the first September Pictorial in 1998. There were 10 of them. They set up their easels in the town and painted the medieval façades of the buildings, the castle, convent, colligate church, and esplanade. At the end of the day, the artists stacked their finished paintings in my living room, against my fireplace, on the window sills, and on top of the furniture. I was a living art gallery. Day after day, the painters sat on their stools in front of their easels and painted the buildings in the old town and the landscape in the surrounding countryside. It was an incredible stroke of luck for me. From where I stand, I can only see the rooftops of the town and have often wondered what was at street level. By looking at the paintings, I was able to see the main street, its arcades, cobblestones, gargoyles, fountains, and even the vegetable market that artists liked to put in their paintings to give them life.

One of the artists brought back a painting of the courtyard of our castle, the Château de Chenaux. Finally, I could see what was inside the castle courtyard. Most of the ancient moat had been filled in with earth and grass, except for a large water basin bordered by Hosta plants. In the paintings, I could see the oldest part of the castle, built of fieldstone in 1297, and the brick towers added later. Another artist painted the front of the collegiate church and its frescos above the door. The artists often finished up their paintings in my garden, which allowed me to watch them work. With its arcades, towers, parapets, machicolations, and medieval façades, our town provided an endless choice of subjects to put on canvas.

The artists were extraordinary people; very professional, disciplined, and nothing at all what I had expected. Their painting supplies were organized in an orderly manner and cleaned at the end of each day with clinical precision. Overhearing the enthusiastic chatter of the artists, my vocabulary took on the words: gouache, gesso, tempura, medium, pastel, perspective, and vanishing point. My rooms smelled of turpentine and linseed oil. After an intensive day of painting, the artists stood around with their glasses of wine, tired and happy, discussing the result of the day's work. I considered myself lucky to be the center of so much talent and beauty.

A vernissage was organized at the end of the week at the Sacred Heart Institute, where the paintings were offered for sale.

To pay the expenses of the artists, including their lodging in my rooms, it was critical that the paintings sold well.

"There were a lot of people at the vernissage," Phyllie remarked. "How did the paintings sell?"

"Like hotcakes," Isabella replied. "We sold them all. People in the old town are commissioning the artists to paint portraits of their houses. Some of the artists will stay on for the public painting contest and participate with the general public."

The painting contest was a grand success. The children had their own category, displayed their masterpieces proudly, and collected their prizes. The city gave 1000 Swiss francs for the best painting and hung it in the town hall.

The next September, artists were invited from Italy and Hungary, and the French showed up again.

"This has turned into a multinational bazaar," Isabella laughed. Switching constantly between French, Italian, and German, she shepherded the groups around the area, organized the vernissages, and sold the paintings. Since the French were back, a pool of French-speaking artists began to accumulate in my interior. One of them was Alain Jamet, who, in addition to other distinctions, was a *peintre d'armée*, a member of an elite military corps of 150 artists created by Napoleon to follow his troops and paint vast canvases of its victories. Victories were painted, regardless of the outcome of the battles. The corps still existed, and Alain Jamet held the rank of Captain.

There had been painting classes in town off and on during the last century. In the early 1930s, my Journal wrote about the well-known artist Eugene Bouvier from Neuchâtel, who had lived in our town and organized exhibitions and painting classes. I overheard Phyllie talking to Alain Jamet.

"There are no painting or drawing classes for adults in our town at this time, " Phyllie said. "Would you be willing to come a week earlier next year and teach a class in drawing and oil painting?"

He agreed, and week-long painting classes became part of our routine in September. The French teachers, Alain and Jean-François, taught oil and watercolor painting and were soon joined by Marie-France, a multi-talented local artist.

Most of the painting was done outdoors, in the town, at the lakeside, or in the vineyards. Every morning, the artists set off in a convoy of cars led by the house Buick station wagon filled with easels, thermoses of coffee, and picnics. The long history of our area provided a vast inventory of buildings to paint.

There were thatched-roof longhouses at the Neolithic village of Gletterens, Roman ruins at Avenches, medieval façades in Morat, Moudon, the *basse ville* (lower town) of Fribourg and the nearby castle of Font. I am fortunate to have been built in an area with such a long history. A time when each building had an identity and no two buildings were alike.

If it rained during the week, the group took refuge under the arcades or in the castle, spreading their paintings out on the bridge over the moat, eating sandwiches, and drinking hot mulled wine. If the weather was too bad, my dining room was set up with a still-life display, and the students sat around the table producing works of variable quality. Oil paintings take time to dry. This presented a problem of where to put them.

A friend of Phyllie's built several large supports that held 10 paintings without touching each other. The frameworks were installed against the wall in my hall, and the participants sat on my stairway studying the effect of their paintings from a distance, wine glass in hand. The bagpipe of Jean-Francois, the watercolor teacher, added a gay ambiance to the evenings.

The September Pictural competition and the painting classes became the major event of the fall season for many years and a favorite of our mayor, who handed out the prizes.

A portrait class was taught in my interior, and everyone in the house became a model. I watched with amusement as they struggled to sit perfectly still for two hours at a time.

Sitting perfectly still was not a problem for me. Over the decade of painting, my portrait was painted from every angle.

My garden, tool shed, and water basin were painted by almost every student and every teacher. My portico with its columns and my ornate gate on Avenue de la Gare were favorite subjects.

The fading sun illuminated my *petit salon* where Phyllie stood gazing at the walls, covered with glorious paintings commemorating this creative period.

"You've become quite famous, haven't you?" she said to me.

"Paintings of you are on the walls of artists and students all over the country and even in France, Italy, and the United States."

They were. I liked to imagine all those people looking at me every day.

My art gallery living room.

A new idea to invigorate our city during the winter had been conceived by Isabella of the tourist office and Christian Gobet, a talented artist who decorates our town and is the cartoonist for the Républicain newspaper. The idea was to create an itinerary of nativity scenes all around the town, displayed between December 4 and January 9. Companies, merchants, hotel owners, and individuals took up the challenge with enthusiasm, and the tourist office shared in the cost.

Materials used came from tree stumps, driftwood from the lake, branches, stones, and objects from garage sales. One surprising creche was made of table and kitchen utensils. Each individual project strived to make something vibrant and alive.

That year 35 different outdoor scenes were displayed and another thirty in churches and shop windows. Visitors and local citizens followed the itinerary on foot or with the *Petit train*.

The director of the Tourist Office was quoted saying,

"It's an event unique in Switzerland. Our town has an incredible pool of creative people, and they want to mark the 2000 years of the Christian era with something special."

Phyllie's colleagues decided I should participate in the event. My gates on Avenue de la Gare were propped open, and a tentlike structure was erected between them that sheltered the holy family. Over the top flew a life-size angel, attached by wires to the tree branches on either side of the gate. Of course, I couldn't see any of the other nativity scenes in town, but I felt sure mine was the most dramatic.

Unfortunately, on the 4th day, a stiff *coup de Joran* blew through my garden, and my angel crashed on top of the holy family.

The short-lived creche was picked up and put away for that year.

~ 20 ~

The rest of the winter was uneventful, and everything was quiet in the neighborhood until March. Then the excitement began.   More than 300 farmers blockaded the ELSA dairy factory demanding a different method of calculation and a higher price for their milk. They claimed the price ELSA paid was 2 to 3 cents lower than major milk buyers such as Swiss Dairy Food, Cremo, or Nestlé. A journalist from La Liberté reported the event blow by blow.

It started at four o'clock in the morning when forty tractors blocked the three accessways to the factory. Warned the night before, the management had stepped up delivery so the last trucks could leave the factory before the blockade. The police arrived at the nearest roundabout at eight, where a group of more than a hundred protesters had lit a bonfire. Half an hour later, the director received a handful of journalists and declared: "I will not give in to blackmail."

The negotiators for the farmers met with the director and his purchasing manager.

"We will not budge. It's all or nothing," said a farmer who had come from as far away as the Jura. Farmers from the districts of Veveyse and Gruyère came to support their colleagues in the Broye.

They carried a banner declaring: "We are not happy farmers."

The factory manager refused to discuss the matter.

The negotiators reported back to the farmers, saying,

"We'll go back in half an hour. Stay calm and don't break anything. Our credibility is at stake."

At eleven o'clock a new meeting was scheduled. "It will be short," the negotiators said.

It was. It only lasted an hour.

Outside, the farmers opened a keg of beer and sliced up a ham. The delegates returned.

"The manager wants us to unblock access to the factory. He has made a small concession, but it's not enough."

While the three delegates returned to negotiate, fifteen farmers headed behind the factory with the idea of closing the gate that opened onto the factory's railway spur, the only exit still open through which two-thirds of the finished product transited. The opposing groups stared at each other in silence.

The police stopped them.

Suddenly, a second group, camouflaged by an embankment, descended on the track where only one policeman was on duty. The factory padlocked the gate. Fifty people were now in front of it. The district commissioner and the police chief conferred with the leaders of the movement. The police chief wanted to interrupt rail traffic to prevent an accident.

The commissioner asked the protesters to move away

from the track, promising they would be told if the factory reopened the gate. One train passed in slow motion, followed by another one. News came from the negotiators.

"There's more progress, but it is still not enough. We're going back for the last time. At 3 'o'clock, we suspend negotiations and resume tomorrow. Everyone will take turns on the picket line."

The farmers pulled out their playing cards, and the local butcher sliced sausages.

The negotiators returned at three-thirty, accompanied by the commissioner and the police chief. The negotiators announced:

"There's a deal...and we can live with it." The blockade was lifted.

I was astonished that this had happened in my own town. It sounded like Margaret Thatcher and the miners' strike in the UK. Being stationary and living in town all of my existence, I had only met one farmer; my neighbor Monsieur Pillonel. I had no idea that farmers were such a dynamic and passionate race.

The early morning sun poked its head over the roof of the ELSA factory and illuminated the back section of my garden.

To my astonishment, I saw a group of people doing gymnastics on the grass, still wet with dew. They soared into the air, stretching their arms high above their heads. When their feet touched back down, a fan of droplets shot out of the grass.

They looked like a collection of Giacometti sculptures in motion. I wasn't accustomed to seeing this much activity so early in the morning. When the exercises were finished, the group gathered around the table in my dining room. Sheet music was passed out by a lyrics teacher. Madame Chung had retired from the National Opera of Paris, and this was her Master Class. Nobody in the house had believed this project would come to life but little did we know the dynamo that was Madame Chung. There was a lot of scrambling around to get the rooms, a full-length mirror, and a classroom prepared. I had observed the new people moving into my rooms the evening before and noticed the cars in my parking lot had French license plates. I heard we were expecting a group of music students, and I was looking forward to having the house resound with music again as it did when my doctor was alive.

This was my first experience with opera singers. One of the objects of the class was to train students to project their voices, without the aid of microphones, in vast outdoor arenas like Avenches, Verona, or Orange. "Projecting your voice," Madame Chung told them, "is like throwing your heart against the wall at the back of the room."

I was soon to find out what that meant. First came the vocalese warm-up exercises. Staccato syllables, ranging from bass to soprano, shot out of a machine gun. The students watched the movements of their mouths in the full-length mirror. In the search for perfection, the vocalese and repetition of high-pitched notes in difficult ranges went on for hours in and out of doors. People passing on Avenue de la Gare stopped with worried looks on their faces, wondering if they should come to the aid of a tortured human or animal. When the exercises came to a merciful end, the students gathered in my *petit salon* around the piano. They were given parts to sing from famous operas. They performed melodious arias from La Traviata, Aïda, Nabucco, and Carmen, paired in groups of three or four. They sang like angels. My rooms have excellent acoustics due to their high ceilings, and my interior resounded with heavenly music.

At the end of the Master Class, Madame Chung organized a concert. The students were dressed in formal evening wear, tuxedos, or long flowing dresses. The students sat serenely in my living room and waited to perform their solos and duets.

One by one, they were presented and took center stage in my *petit salon* next to the piano. In my dining room, the tables had been folded up and replaced by rows of chairs. Phyllie sat on a pillow on my stairway along with others who knew where the best sonority was to be found. All eighty seats were filled, and everyone was overjoyed. The concert ended with the students singing Offenbach's Barcarolle from the Tales of Hoffmann. The audience joined hands and filed out into the garden for the intermission and refreshments. It reminded me of the musical program organized in my garden by Jacqueline Thévoz in the 50s. I was pleased to be the center of all this talent and beauty once again.

For the five wonderful years that the Master Class continued, we enjoyed the company of these sensitive and talented singers. Our concerts became well-known in the town, and I looked forward to the return of the Master Class with anticipation every year.

Master class opera.

The students were very advanced with a lot of concert experience. In addition to analyzing their voice, posture, breathing, and interpretation, the Master Class helped them penetrate the maze of obstacles between them and the hermetic opera companies.

One of the years, the fourth I think, Madame Chung sat in my salon and said to Phyllie, "I'm not satisfied with the level of my students this year. I am going to invite a few friends from Paris to come and join them for the concert to bolster the level."

Internationally known opera performers arrived before the concert, and we were treated to an unforgettable lyrical performance. I was bursting with pride to have such outstanding talent in my interior. The Opera Festival in Avenches was running simultaneously. Those in the audience who had been to both my concert and Avenches agreed that the event in my *petit salon* was the most inspiring.

I was sad when the Master Class came to an end. It had been my favorite event during the year. Over a cup of coffee, Madame Chung asked Phyllie,

"Would you like to come to Paris? Bring your friends. I will have the régisseur of the Palais Garnier give you a tour."

"Would you really? Of course, we will come."

And they did. The Palais Garnier has been called "probably the most famous opera house in the world," a symbol of Paris like Notre Dame Cathedral, the Louvre, or the Sacré Coeur Basilica. Phyllie and her friends visited Madame Chung's former dressing room, the Nureyev ballet studio, the costume-making workshop with its ceiling covered with suspended tutus, the backstage handlers with their complex network of pullies, ropes and marine terminology, and the underground water-course. Naturally, a lot of photos were taken, and I saw the Palais Garnier once again. I had seen it and other famous buildings in Paris in the *Illustration* magazines in 1912. The Palace, the Cathedral, the Louvre, and the Basilica looked just the same now as they did then. The best thing about classical structures like those and like me is that we don't age, and we don't go out of style.

~ 21 ~

I had lived through blackouts during the second world war, and I never expected to do it again. Suddenly in 1999, I was plunged into total darkness. Mon Dieu! What's going on? Finally, my lights, connected to an outside source, came back on. All my fuses had been blown. There were cables and wires along my hallway and a string of hot spotlights, 600 watts each. No wonder my fuses blew out.

When I could see again, I saw people walking around in my living room, reciting lines in Swiss German. My interior was filled with actors, cameramen, technicians, make-up people, and someone was yelling, "LIGHTS, CAMERA, ACTION, CUT."

I discovered that I had become the on-site location of the popular Swiss television soap opera entitled Lüthi und Blanc.

The series was about a family who owned a chocolate factory, and the plot was full of intrigue; a Swiss Dallas, complete with heroes and villains. I became quite famous during that time. The episodes covered family intrigues, bankruptcy, succession, love affairs, in-laws, banking schemes in Zurich, and conspiracies in the family bar in the Tessin. An effort had been made to spread the story over all the linguistic parts of Switzerland. I was the Villa Blanc in the French-speaking part of the story. I liked the idea that Americans thought I was the White House, not knowing that Blanc, in this case, was a 205 family name, not a color. The actors were Hans Heinz Moser, the principal actor in a German TV series, and Linda Geiser, a charming and interesting person who lived in New York and flew in to perform in the series.

The film crew had first discovered me when one of them came for a bed-and-breakfast weekend. I remembered him saying to his companion, "This is exactly the kind of house the director is looking for. I'll take some pictures and show them to her on Monday." I was surprised when the B&B guest came back with several others later in the week and asked to take my front door off and take it to Bülach. It was a chilly April day, and Phyllie flatly refused. They photographed my door, entry, living room, and staircase and reproduced it all on a sound stage in Bülach. They painted a replica of my marble mosaic hallway on the floor of their set. After the initial shock, I got used to them coming to film. They were either a few people or a crew of 30 with cameras on rails and vehicles of all kinds. On entering my hall, one of the new film crew members remarked, "It looks just like our set in Bülach."

When the filming segments were completed in the replica of my interior in Bülach, the cast came to me on-site to connect the episodes. The actors went up and downstairs, in and out of my front door, twenty or thirty times.

They repeatedly opened and shut windows, ran in and out of the gate, and sometimes filmed actors in my garden.

Filming session for the soap opera Lüthi und Blanc

There was a rainy-day scene under my sequoia tree, where the actor stood stoically while he was sprayed with water and recited his lines soaking wet. My proximity to the train station presented a problem for filming outdoor scenes. Filming had to be interrupted every four or five minutes for the passage of freight trains from the ELSA factory. Since Migros was one of the sponsors of the series, they were asked to send someone to the site and provide a schedule for freight traffic. The problem was not resolved when the filming came to an end.

In the script, the chocolate factory of the Blanc Family was located in St. Croix. Each time the crew came to film, they took down my city flag and put one up from the State of Vaud, where St. Croix is located. For seven years, the film crew became an integral part of our crowded agenda. When the series ended in 2007 after 200 episodes, the producer gave Phyllie two sacks of video cassettes, covering the episodes. I missed the spotlights, the technicians, the actors, and of course, the notoriety. In my starring role as The Villa Blanc, I had become quite well known. It was fun to be famous and watch the program come on the TV with an opening shot of my front door. Now that the series was finished, I would have to adjust to a more modest lifestyle.

Modest is not my favorite word.

Two teachers from the secondary school conceived the last project in my cultural period. It was an English vacation for their students recreated in my interior with English-only conversation, British films, and fish and chips. The music of The Beatles echoed throughout my rooms. Words were stuck all over the house, noting the name of the object. I became accustomed to seeing CUPBOARD stuck in my kitchen, SINK in the bathroom, and CURTAIN pinned in the living room. When English week was over, the class sent me a picture and a thank you note, which I thought was very nice of them, even if it was addressed to Phyllie.

Autumn had come, and I was admiring the crimson color of my maple trees on Avenue de la Gare when a sugar beet rolled up to my gate. A wagon had broken a trailer hitch, overturned, and covered the street with sugar beets. A little excitement is always welcome on Avenue de la Gare. Traffic was disrupted for an hour and delayed a delivery truck with a large wooden crate addressed to me. Phyllie opened the crate and closed it again immediately. She was going to need help with this consignment. Friends were invited for the holidays and supplied the necessary manpower to tackle the crate. After a day of digging out solidified building foam bit by bit, a life-size museum copy of a terracotta warrior from the Xian excavation emerged. He was placed in the corner of my living room. I really felt quite intimidated and hoped we were not going to keep him long. One must not expect flexibility from buildings. Rigidity is our best quality.

The arrival of the Chinese warrior was a consequence of the stopover of two bed-and-breakfast guests during the summer vacation. At the breakfast table, I overheard Phyllie and Rosmarie talking to them. The couple had stayed a week in my Cedar Room. I liked them because they thought I had a special atmosphere, a compliment I never tired of hearing. They lived in China. During break-fast, they invited Phyllie to come to visit them. I knew from my early education derived from the Illustration magazines that China was someplace very far away. I expected Phyllie to decline the invitation politely. At that time, China was not a common destination for Europeans. But instead, she turned to Rosmarie and asked, "Will you come with me?"

And off they went to China. When they came back, I heard all about China, the Great Wall, etc. etc. In the photos, I saw the Forbidden City, a complex of 980 buildings, all of them red. There's a lot of red in China. The palace had a nice roof and some unusual drain pipes.

"It's 611 years old," they said.

I wasn't impressed. By now, our castle was over 700 years old. They visited the B&B guests who lived outside of Shanghai and then went to Xian to see the excavation of the army of terracotta warriors. And now, one of them sat in my living room.

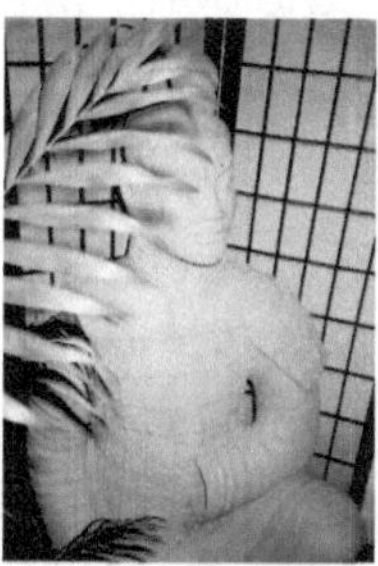

**The warrior of
Emperor Qin.**

Fortunately, the warrior wasn't too ferocious-looking, and little by little, I became accustomed to seeing him there in the corner. His head and his hands were not attached. There had been an unhelpful datasheet explaining that in Chinese.

The warrior was occasionally lent to the Laténium museum in Neuchâtel for exhibitions. That bit of gravitas made me more receptive to him, and over time, I finally came to be proud of having a representative of Emperor Qin in the corner of my living room.

Phyllie had spent a lot of time on the organization of my cultural period. Whereas I did appreciate that effort, my maintenance had been neglected, and my renovation program was behind schedule. She sat in the living room, now shared by the warrior of Emperor Qin, and stared at the ceiling. It was time for one of our sunset monologues. I waited to hear what she had to say.

"It's about that depressing dark green color in the hall and up the stairs," she said.

"I want to repaint it, but I don't know how to do the faux marble panels on the bottom."

She thought for a while and continued.

" I'll start with the walls. The height of the stairwell is going to be a problem. To get up to the vaulted ceiling, I could put part of my scaffolding on the first floor and the rest on the landing of the stairs, then bridge the two with those long picnic tables in the basement. That would give me a working platform five and a half meters off the floor.

I should be able to reach all parts of the walls and ceiling like that."

Was she kidding? It sounded suicidal to me. Assuming she survived the operation, what color was she planning to paint my walls and faux marble panels? "There's a nice apricot color in the mosaic on the floor," she continued.

"I think that would be suitable and much more cheerful than that sinister dull green. The antique fair at Landeron opens next weekend. I could probably find a specialist in faux marble there."

An artist was indeed found in Landeron and came to work with Phyllie on the project. Together, they started with the panels in the hall at floor level. In the beginning, they shared one palette, the artist mixing the colors. As Phyllie became more skilled, they worked side by side.

When they got cramps in their legs, they moved to panels going up the stairs where they could work seated on the steps. The mixture of linseed oil, turpentine, and pigment had to be just right, or the composition didn't stick. If there was too much oil, it slid off the wall. The last touch was a bit of white to add depth. Long after the 55 panels were finished, I discovered that one had been forgotten on the first floor. I was annoyed by this mistake at first, but as time when on, I came to accept it as a historical reference to the old and new faux marble panels.

I was happy with the result. My intrepid owner glued a Navaho vase in the corner on the highest part of the stairwell as a souvenir of the undertaking. When the scaffolding came down and the picnic tables were put back in the basement, my entry hall was both cheerful and grandiose. Another improvement came soon after that.

When my foundation was laid in 1911, it was divided into seven rooms, all with load-bearing walls to support the floors above. There was a furnace room, two storage rooms, a pool room, a potting cellar, a laundry room, and a workshop.

I was well satisfied with these elements until Phyllie organized a few wine tasting sessions in my living room. A society of Swiss winegrowers from the Lavaux vineyards came and brought brochures and pictures of their wine cellars with them. It reminded me of my early days when I looked at the Illustration magazines from Paris. In the Illustration, I saw castles in the Bordeaux and Burgundy areas of France, and they all had wine cellars they were very proud of in their basements.

I had tried to put it out of my mind. One should not dwell on things that are out of one's reach. Jack had been a wine connoisseur and read books with pictures of dim, musty, wonderfully mysterious cellars filled with bottles in horizontal racks from floor to ceiling. The windows in these cellars were composed of round amber circles of glass held together by lead. How I would have loved to have a wine cellar with windows like that.

Winter arrived again, and this time brought with it a friend from Washington state. Being a wine lover, he and Phyllie spent long evenings over a glass of wine, discussing the merits of the sun-drenched California production of Chardonnay, Cabernet Sauvignon et Merlot. Phyllie defended our unique Swiss white wines made from the Chasselas grape and promised her visitor a tour of the Lavaux vineyards on Lake Leman to show him the difficulty of producing wine on almost vertical terrain.

"I'm surprised there isn't a wine cellar in a house like this," Vern, our visitor, said.

"I know," Phyllie replied. "I think one must have been planned. There's a place for it in the basement that's perfect. I'll show you."

He was shown the small storage room between my laundry room and workshop. One side of the room had wooden cabinets already built-in for storing preserves.

"It really is perfect," Vern said. "I have a little bit of time on this trip. Let's do it."

I was overjoyed to hear this. I did like this man.

They took on the project with enthusiasm. They found diamond-shaped wine rack modules and screwed them to the wall from the floor to the ceiling. A large wooden barrel that had sat for years in my workshop found its place against the wall of the wine cellar and proudly displayed a collection of pewter jugs called channes. A rustic wood-and-wrought-iron ceiling light that never fit anywhere in the house was perfect for the cellar. The somber light that good wine prefers was created by using 15-watt oven-proof light bulbs. Rosmarie came by to see how the project was getting on.

"You make stain glass windows," Phyllie said,

"Is it possible to replace the glass in this cellar window with amber bottle glass?"

"I could give it a try," she replied.

Phyllie had no idea what she was asking for.

Some weeks later, Rosmarie turned up with the two magnificent amber-leaded glass window panels.

They were beautiful. I was overjoyed.

"How did you do it?"

"Well," Rosmarie replied. "At the Musée du Vitrail (stained glass museum) in Romont, I found a book on how to make bull's eye window panels. Near Zurich, I found a supplier of "Butzenscheiben," as the Germans call these amber-colored hand-blown glass circles, along with some flat glass the same color, for the spaces in-between. Then, I edged each glass circle with a special lead and fitted the flat glass between them. After reinforcing the whole assembly, I fitted it into the window frame.

"Wow!" Phyllie was speechless.

The window panes were installed, and they were superb. The last stage was covering the concrete floor with gravel and then buying wine. I can't tell you how delighted I was with my wine cellar. It was atmospheric and captivating, and I had no reason to be envious of the castles in France.

Vern had gone back to Washington state, and Phyllie sat in her chair in the living room. The shadows lengthened as the sun dropped behind the Jura.

"It was wonderful having Vern here, wasn't it? And thanks to him, you finally have a wine cellar."

Yes, I thought. I was pleased with that. I wondered what she going to do next.

"I've been thinking about the basement of the annex," she said. The new sport of mountain biking had become popular in our area. Mountain bikes with fat tires and 21 gears were appearing throughout the countryside and in the forests. The local dairy factory organized an annual cyclocross competition called the Elsa Bike Trophy that attracted more than a thousand participants each year. It was a two-day event, and competitors booked rooms early at my Bed and Breakfast. The weather was often rainy, and the cyclists appeared on my doorstep covered with mud from head to toe.

"I've been thinking about making a studio apartment in the basement with a shower," Phyllie said. "The cyclists could shower before coming into the house, and it would also function as a classroom." Naturally, not being fond of mud, I approved of this idea. The basement, however, housed three automobiles; a Ferrari, a Maserati, and a Datsun. What was she going to do with them?

"I'll have to sell the cars," she said.

That was going to be difficult for her. So many memories of Jack were connected to those elegant, fast cars. It was an emotional moment when the cars were sold, and Phyllie didn't have the courage to be present the day they were towed away. I watched sadly as the cars were loaded on a flat-bed truck and disappeared down my driveway.

Sixty years ago, my basement had been a physiotherapy room with lots of torturous-looking machines where patients labored to improve their health. The linoleum installed on the floor in 1937 had disintegrated and fused into the concrete slab beneath it.

It had to be chipped out, centimeter by centimeter. Phyllie's colleagues, who were accustomed to difficult excavations, came to help. The space cut out of the wall to move the cars in was walled up again. A fold-up bed was fixed to the wall to make the room suitable both as a classroom and living space. My physiotherapy room/ former garage/now studio was ready for teachers, and the cyclists had a shower. I liked its cheerful yellow and blue provincial décor and its matching stained glass window.

My renovation program was now up to date. My structure was not going to require any more attention for a long time.

At least, that's what I thought.

The year, the decade and the millennium were coming to an end. One could reasonably expect special events to occur, but I could never have imagined the disaster the end of the year would bring.

~ 22 ~

On the day after Christmas 1999, the weather was chilly, nothing unusual. The temperature of my foundation predicted nothing other than an ordinary winter day. With no warning at all, I was hit by a devastating hurricane with over 200-kilometer-an- hour winds, unknown in recorded Swiss meteorological history. The hurricane was named Lothar. Phyllie had returned from Austria on the morning of the drama. That was fortunate for the guest family who had rented my rooms for the holiday and wouldn't have to face the ordeal alone.

Full-grown trees fell like matchsticks in the path of the hurricane as it swept along my west side. Several fell on top of the cars in my parking lot. I could feel my wooden shutters being yanked off their hinges and flung to the ground. My recently replaced copper drain pipes were ripped from the roof and twisted like licorice sticks. The fire department arrived immediately. From a distance, they had seen the trees falling. To my horror, a man from the guest family was out in the garden at the height of the storm, calmly filming the trees as they fell.

All of a sudden, there was a great thud that jolted me to

the base of my foundation. The cedar, now a massive towering tree that I had grown up with and had stood by me faithfully for almost a century, was twisted off its trunk

by a 220-kilometer vortex and smashed through my roof and walls. Heavy branches pierced the newly painted wall of my blue room, where children were playing with their toys. Snow and rain came through the roof. For the first time, I understood what it was like to have my structure penetrated by a projectile and thought of all the buildings demolished by bombs during the wars.

The rental family, who demonstrated incredibly solid nerves, were moved down to the first floor. As the hurricane swept across Europe, they reasoned it wouldn't strike twice in the same place and decided to wait it out with me. A few days later, they packed up and took their children to the mountains.

The note they left saying "their stay had been unforgettable" is displayed in our visitor's album.

The hurricane ended as suddenly as it had begun. An eerie silence followed the dropping of the wind, punctuated by the sound of cracking limbs and ambulance sirens. The destruction left behind was heartbreaking. My first-floor balcony was demolished. It was sad to see my rooms filled with wet branches and debris after all the work that had been done to renovate them.

The hurricane followed a narrow trajectory that took out all the trees on my west side and continued to take the roof off the church and the tower of the castle. Nine trees in my garden had been uprooted or broken off, and my orchard was completely wiped out. Our area was so hard hit, I had to wait a long time for repairmen to come to my aid. The insurance estimator came and explained that I was a lower priority than houses that had no roofs at all.

He told us about a roof from one house that had been lifted off and set down on top of the neighbor's house where two elderly people were watching television with their headphones, completely unaware of the squatting second roof. After the initial shock and copious tears, my furniture was moved out of the second-floor rooms into the hall. Workmen covered the roof with a tarp and, Phyllie being unable to do anything else, left for Arizona. It was a depressing episode for me, left alone in the dark, with a hole in my roof, branches in my rooms, and freezing temperatures.

By the end of February, repairs were finally underway. There was a lot of sawing, chopping, and wood hauling going on around me. The lovely magnolia tree, smashed by the falling cedar, was pruned severely without much hope for its survival.

My balcony and part of my roof were replaced against a background rhythm of chainsaws, sanders, and nail guns. The modern synthetic materials used to repair my interior walls felt strange and unfamiliar against my traditional structure. I was not reassured by the lightweight foam substrate being attached to my walls. It felt like a layer of whipped cream rather than the substantial lath and plaster I was accustomed to. I was particularly sad to see the broken-off cedar tree, and I wondered what would happen to it. Phyllie understood that the cedar tree held a special significance for me. She sat in my living room as the sun went down, and after a period of silence, she said,

"It's a pity about the cedar tree. I saw some pictures in the Républicain this week of wonderful sculptures made with a chainsaw. The paper says the artist doesn't want to be solicited, but I'll talk to Monsieur Borcard at the Républicain and see if he'll tell me who he is."

I thought it was nice of her to be so sensitive and aware of my feelings. Instead of removing what was left of the cedar tree, she had it cut off a meter from the ground. The artist, a local man with a large farm to manage, was weary of being petitioned for his sculptures.

"I know how busy you must be, " Phyllie said on the telephone.

"I only wanted to ask if you have ever carved a cedar tree?"

After a long silence, the farmer answered.

"No, but I understand it carves like butter and smells wonderful."

The farmer with the soul of an artist was captivated by the setting. In one afternoon, he carved the stump into a sculpture of two bears, using a large chain saw and a smaller one for the finishing touches. My gate opening onto Avenue de la Gare was left open for the artist's family to enter and see the sculpture. The whole neighborhood smelled pleasantly of fresh cedar wood.

I have some scars from Lothar that I will bear for the rest of my existence. We were not the only country affected. The storm devastated large areas in France, Germany, and Italy. Winds hit a record 272 kilometers an hour, 140 people were killed, and the damage was estimated at 10 billion euros.

When our bed-and-breakfast season began, guests were limited to the first floor. Six months later, when my second floor was functional again, I turned the page on this somber episode and moved into the new millennium.

The shrill ring of the telephone resonated around my interior. It was Phyllie's son calling from California. On the speakerphone, the young man sounded terribly shaken.

"Have you heard yet, Mom? Airplanes have attacked New York. So far, two skyscrapers have been demolished. I don't know if more planes are on the way. It's like something from outer space."

September 11th would remain in public memory as the most devastating terrorist attack in contemporary history.

Turning on the local television channel, we learned that terrorists had hijacked four commercial airliners, crashing two into the Twin Towers in New York and one into the Pentagon. The fourth plane targeted the White House, but passengers fought the hijackers, and it crashed into a field. The world was in shock. Along with everyone around me, I was sad and fearful.

We learned that the assault had been perpetrated by a radical Islamic terror organization bent on destroying our way of life.

That day, an American flag was put on the flag-pole installed in my front yard by Jack's colleagues from Zurich. Phyllie lowered it to half-mast and went back inside, forgetting to shut my gate that opens onto Avenue de la Gare. I watched a steady stream of people come and go all day through my open gate.

When Phyllie came back outside, she was surprised to see a pile of flowers, almost half a meter high, encircling the flagpole.

This touching gesture of solidarity from the local population for the suffering of a far-away nation brought tears to her eyes.

The year after that, the 6th Swiss National Exhibition opened. It was divided into five sites called Arteplages, located in Neuchâtel, Yverdon-les-Bains, Morat, Bienne, and on a traveling barge representing the Jura. The Soroptimists, a charitable women's group, rented all my rooms and held a lovely candle-light dinner on my tennis court. These remarkable women supported numerous humanitarian projects and were very enthusiastic about the Expo. Auguste Piccard's bathyscaph was on display in Morat, along with a temporary rust-colored monolith floating in the lake. Inside this spacious building, visitors had the privilege of viewing the monumental historical painting of the June 22, 1476 Battle of Morat, painted by Louis Braun in the year 1893. Sadly, when the exposition ended, this magnificent panorama was rolled up and put back into obscurity in military storage.

In our little kingdom, I could sense that change was on the horizon. For some time, a gentleman had been appearing in my interior. He was tall and slender with grey hair and an aristocratic bearing. I had even seen him cooking in my kitchen. Fifteen years had gone by since Jack had passed away, and maybe Phyllie was getting tired of being a widow.

She sat in my living room by the fireplace as the sun was setting. I knew she had something to tell me, and I was quite sure I knew what it was.

"I have decided to remarry," she said.

"I'm going to marry Frédéric de Martini. I imagine you will approve of his social status. He comes from a very old ennobled family who, among other things, built cars in St. Blaise at the beginning of the last century."

I remembered those beautiful Martini cars passing on Avenue de la Gare in the '20s. In fact, my neighbor Charles Bovet had one. My owner didn't know it, but I had observed Monsieur de Martini closely for several months. I knew he was a widower and retired from the government in Bern. He had willingly helped in the garden and undertook repairs on my structure, which I had taken note of and appreciated. After considerable reflection, I decided that I approved of him, but I had the feeling that Phyllie was holding something back.

I waited.

"Well," she said finally, "he has a house of his own."

Mais...mais ça ne va pas !

I was shocked. Devastated. What did it mean? Was she going to leave me? Surely the house of Monsieur de Martini was not more beautiful than I. Surely, he would get rid of it and come to live in me.

Phyllie continued. "We will continue to live here, except in the winter. Then we will be in his farmhouse in the country.

It's not far away. It has a wood stove and is cozy in the winter.

I'll come twice a week to see that you're alright."

Cozy! I'm grand and elegant, and she wants cozy?

And what about Madame Chung's Master Class, the Septembre Pictural, the painting classes, the American students, the soap opera, and the bed-and-breakfast guests. All of those people needed her. Had she thought of them? Had she?

"The cultural programs will continue just as they do now," she said.

"Now that the studio is finished, the teachers have a separate classroom during the day and a comfortable apartment at night."

Finally, I calmed down. I guess it wouldn't be so bad after all. The wedding took place in our castle, as civil weddings do in our town. From the photos, I could finally see the interior of the castle. There is a lovely baroque room reserved for marriage ceremonies. The wedding reception was held in my dining and living rooms. After a short honeymoon, the new husband settled into our intense routine as best he could. When the vocalese of the Master Class became too shrill, the turpentine of the painting class too smelly, the American students too noisy, or he found himself tripping over the cables of the film crew, he took refuge in the peaceful environment of his own house in the country.

My beloved neighbor, the Bellevue Hotel, later the Institute Stavia, was exactly a hundred years old that year. That should have been a reason to celebrate, but alas, it was just the opposite. The school closed and a bank foreclosed on the building. For nearly a century, I had watched tourists and students come and go through the main entrance of this extraordinary edifice and linger in its garden across from my front gate. Even though the institute was still functioning, the bank wanted to take it off its books. The difficulty of adapting it to a new function and the constraints of being a protected building had condemned The Bellevue to remain empty and deteriorate. This bit of human illogic frightens me, and I hope the same fate will not befall me.

Another spring was well on its way. The yellow *bouton d'or* poked their heads through the snow, and I could feel my façade starting to warm up. Easter and the Surrexit procession were followed by the arrival of the cherry blossoms and the American students from the University of Georgia. One morning after the final exams, they came down to breakfast dressed in togas. They had taken the sheets off their beds, draped them around their bodies, and tied a knot at the shoulder. It was hilarious. The sheets in my bedrooms are the flowered Laura Ashley sort. That year, the study program had concentrated on the Roman Empire. It had been an intensive period of study with architectural layouts, Latin inscriptions, battle strategy, and final exams. The tired students must have felt the need for some comic relief.

Their program grew more intensive every year and

included trips to France, Spain, and Scotland. The Studies Abroad program, as it was called, occasionally coincided with the medieval festivals held in our town.

This was an opportunity for the students to discover the food and customs of the Middle Ages.

They helped with the preparations, covered modern advertising signs with jute, turned the spit roasting a whole pig in the street, and set up a bar selling hydromel, a wine made from honey. Dressing in medieval costumes was fun, especially for the girls who spent a long time choosing their dresses and dancing around my living room. It was a marvelous sight to see these modern, sophisticated young Americans leave the house in their long dresses and belted tunics, halberds at the ready, heading straight for the Middle Ages.

As time passed, I was struggling to adapt my vocabulary to the new technology of the students. I was now hearing:

iPhone, iPad, GPS, modems, drones, tablets, Google, Skype, social media, Facebook, and Twitter. I didn't think these smartphones would become popular because they were so expensive, but I had underestimated the human obsession with technology.

The students, who had traveled a great distance to learn the ways of other cultures, sat in my entry closest to the modem and talked to their families and friends on Skype.

At the breakfast table one morning, I listened to Phyllie discussing the student program with the professor.

"We started this program to broaden the horizons of our students by cutting them off from their environment and putting them in another culture. And until now, it worked.

With Skype, iPhones, and social media, isolation is no longer possible. Our program, as we conceived it, is going to be difficult to sustain in the future."

You're right," said the professor. "Ancient history defeated by modern electronics. What a pity."

And with that, my academic career ended. My cultural period also came to a close with the last edition of the painting contest and a complimentary event with poetry and music held in a gate tower in the ramparts, opened once a year for the occasion. I would miss the canvases stacked in my hall, the smell of turpentine, and the animated chatter of our little artist colony. A surprising number of talented artists had been discovered among the population in our area. I was proud to have fulfilled a role in promoting the visual arts, just like the famous artist colonies at Montmartre and Barbizon...well, sort of. A figure from my past turned up that summer. It was Jacqueline Thévoz who had orchestrated the dancing classes in my garden 50 years ago. Phyllie was in her chair and talking to me that evening.

"Jacqueline Thévoz came by. She brought me a red scrapbook with pictures of the girls who danced in the garden in 1947. Of course, you saw that, didn't you? That must have been lovely."

It was.

"I'm afraid I didn't realize what a famous person she was and all she had done in the field of art, music, journalism, composition, and film. It was a pity I missed the opportunity to get to know this exceptional woman better."

It was. Of course, I knew her well. I had wonderful memories of little girls flitting through my garden like fairies to the music of Jean Binet. I wondered what she was going to do with the scrapbook.

"I'll give the scrapbook to one of the girls in the photos. It shouldn't be difficult to find them."

The conversation ended with the arrival of our neighbor, Monsieur Pillonel. His mill was being put into operation for visitors, and he came to invite Phyllie to see it. The millstones were chiseled in the department of the Seine et Marne in France.

In 2000, a group called Swiss Mill Friends had been created to preserve the mills for future generations and to pass on the know-how of milling. The association had

450 members and published an annual guide. The

Moulin Pillonel was one of four mills open to the public that year. Unfortunately, I could only observe it from a distance.

I was not left out of the event in April 2010. On a cloudy day, thousands of spectators held their breath on the tarmac of the Payerne Airport as the single-seated monoplane powered only by solar panels lifted slowly off the tarmac for its first 24-hour flight. The Piccard family of explorers was back.

Bertrand Piccard, teamed with André Borschberg, was taking the first step in an around-the-world flight using only solar power. Five years later, their expedition took off from the United Arab Emirates on its first leg. Some delays were experienced when the aircraft's batteries were damaged flying over the Pacific Ocean and took months to repair. Over a 16 month period, Solar Impulse flew 42,000-kilometres of a multi-stage journey around the world to promote clean energy technology.

I had become accustomed to seeing the solar airplane floating soundlessly over my roof during its test flights. Although its shape was different, it reminded me of the noiseless Graf Zeppelin dirigible that had passed overhead in 1930.

It was always a pleasure to hear the sound of the postman's motorbike and hear the plop of the newspaper dropping into my mailbox. A welcome article in Le Républicain announced that our venerable steamboat would be returning to Lake Neuchâtel. Our paddle steamer, Neuchâtel, inaugurated on May 9, 1912, was going to be restored and put back into service. I had always loved to hear the mournful blast of its foghorn as it came toward our port and the steady chug chug it made as it moved to the dock. In 1913, the Neuchâtel provided daily service from Bienne to Neuchâtel, while an identical boat, the Fribourg, connected to Yverdon. Unfortunately, this attractive offer ended the following year because of the war. The Neuchâtel is a lake and river steamer, unlike the other steamers on Swiss lakes. The height limitations of bridges on the canals of La Broye and La Thiele led to some original innovations. The main salon was built into the hull, the smokestack could be tilted, and the air vents had removable sleeves. In 1969, the Neuchâtel was taken out of service and transformed into a restaurant docked in the port of Neuchâtel. In 1999, she was put up for sale. Trivapor, an association for steam navigation, was set up to acquire the steamboat and turn it back into an operational steamer. After long negotiations with the real estate firm that owned it, Trivapor bought the Neuchâtel on February 22, 2007. Private donors, the Loterie Romande, the States of Neuchâtel and Vaud, neighboring municipalities, and the Federal Office of Culture financed the renovation.

The historic steamer left Neuchâtel on September 18th, 2010, on its way to Morat, via the Canal de la Broye and finally reached Sugiez where it would be restored. Escorted by a police launch on one side and the barge Attila of the company TSM Perrottet on the other, the extraordinary convoy set off at 10 a.m., made a celebratory stopover in Morat, and arrived the next day at the shipyard of Sugiez. Steamboat fans were able to follow the convoy aboard a boat chartered for the occasion. The technical department of the *Société de navigation du lac des Quatre-Cantons* super-vised the delicate operation of moving the 150-ton boat into dry dock using a giant crane.

After a turbulent history of coal shortages during the war, the loss of cubic meters of water under its hull due to the three-lake water management scheme, and changing owners four times, we looked forward again to the wel-come sound of our paddle steamer's foghorn as it pulled into our port.

It wasn't the only good news Le Républicain brought us. A new theater was opening up in our neighborhood. Our Casino-Théâtre, built-in 1902, had made our town famous all over Switzerland with its production of "A travers le vieux Stavayé."

For so many years, I enjoyed watching adults lining up to get into performances at the Casino-Théâtre and chil-dren waiting impatiently for the matinees. The new, cozy little theater called the Azimut was just across the street from me. It would be putting on plays, films, conferences, and concerts throughout the year. With the revival of the Neuchâtel steamboat and our new neighborhood theater, I had the feeling that some of the charm of the Belle Epoque of my youth was coming back.

I wasn't the only one reminiscing about the old days. The industrialization of my neighborhood had begun in 1924 with the expansion of the Moulin Agricole and had gone unchecked since. It seemed that nothing could slow the advance of voracious industrialists as they covered the land, acre by acre, with cement. But something did. Feel-ing threatened by industrial expansion, seventeen farmers united to create the Broye Agricultural Land Protection Group to defend their agricultural land. The association was open to all farmers in the district. The Fribourg Chamber of Agriculture, who supported the group, said,

"A partnership between developers and farmers is fundamental."

The battle was rude. More than 1,000 jobs were expected to be created by industrial projects that threatened fifty hectares of agricultural land. According to a local farmer, if the present trend continued, "in 200 years, there will be no more agriculture in the area." The association succeeded in being recognized and consulted before and during any new project. The farmers knew that development was inevitable but wanted it to be as harmonious as possible. They said, "They didn't want their farms to become vegetable patches in the middle of an industrial zone."

It wasn't the only local conflict. The Port of Estavayer constructed by the sailing club in 1969 was constantly improved, functioned profitably, and provided a valuable service to the community. The original 40-year concession granted by the State of Fribourg had expired, and the City of Estavayer wanted to take over the port, adding another conflict to our much-disputed shoreline. Bitter legal battles ensued, and the port, like the chalets in the Grand Cariçaie, became valuable clients of the prosperous legal firms in the area.

By then, a huge share of retail business had been taken over by The Internet. Customers who had shopped in stores were now shopping online. Internet shopping was squeezing out the shopping centers, which had squeezed out family businesses before them. In 1924 when photography became part of our life, catalogs were coming in the mail from other countries displaying products at bargain prices. Our local authorities warned that it was unwise to order things by mail. It was recommended that the population *buy local* and support the businesses in our community. We were now being told that again. After years of rampant importation of food from the far corners of the earth, consumers were returning to locally grown produce.

The year 2011 brought good news for the 108 naturalized frogs eating spaghetti, playing pool, and getting a haircut in our museum. The frogs housed there were now 160 years old, which is old for anything, especially a frog. A credit was allotted by the community to restore them.

"More than a third of them are in very bad shape," explained Cholé Maquelin, a restorer from the Museum of Ethnography in Neuchâtel commissioned to assess the health of each specimen.

"Their skin has deteriorated. It has become brittle, almost like glass. Some have cracks in their bodies or dislocated limbs. Floor vibrations resulting from the passage of thousands of visitors day after day has emptied the sand that filled the frogs' bodies."

Using X-rays, she was able to find the best way to proceed with the restoration; however, she warned that it was unlikely they could all be saved.

~ 23 ~

I will never forget the winter of 2012, the worst one in 30 years. Thick buildups of ice amassed on the trees, cars, and buildings. The weight of the ice sank boats in the harbors. The Siberian temperatures made the lake look like it was smoking.

Fishermen were unable to work and had to be subsidized. Ice skaters invaded the shores of the lake and skated without interruption from the port to the Grand Gouille, weaving in and out of the reeds that jutted up through the ice. My owners went off to Arizona and left me alone and empty. I was freezing and not very happy with them. My windows were completely opaque, covered with a thick layer of frost. I looked like an ice palace. Fortunately for me, Margot came and turned up the heat, and put pillows against my windows. I was lucky to escape with only one frozen radiator.

Summer came and went, and it was already 2014. A hundred years had passed since the start of World War I, but there was no longer anyone around who remembered that. Phyllie was struggling with our overcrowded agenda. In the midst of the summer vacation period, there was not much time for a leisurely chat with her. I saw her in her chair by the fireplace. I could tell she was worried about something. I waited for her to tell me what it was.

"It will soon be the Opera festival at the amphitheater in Avenches," she said.

"They're doing Carmen this year, and the role of Micaëla is being sung by Greta Baldwin, a well-known American soprano."

So..., why was she telling me this?

"Well, she and her family are booked here. I am afraid they'll be disappointed when they see we're just a modest guesthouse. An imperial diva like that is probably used to five-star hotels. I can't imagine her sharing the bathroom. I shouldn't have taken the reservation," she fretted.

I was a bit put out with Phyllie. I didn't consider myself a 'modest guesthouse,' and I didn't see why an imperial diva should be different from anyone else. Had she forgotten Nicoletta, the famous french singer who stayed with us during her concert at the Abbatial in Payerne?

I kept an eye out for the arrival of the 'diva.' Guests for the Opera Festival were arriving and settling in when a young woman in jeans, sweatshirt, and ponytail rang my doorbell.

"I'm Greta Baldwin," she said. "My family are reserved here and will be coming along soon."

Her warm and friendly family stayed the week of the Opera Festival. Greta was the sweetest, most unassuming young lady we had ever had among our guests. She seemed completely unaware of the beauty and talent she possessed. At the breakfast table the morning after her performance, everyone agreed that Greta stole the show. Unfortunately, I didn't hear her sing, but the guests did. Phyllie said *she left us with the memory of an unforgettable aria that floated over our ancient amphitheater and the gracious young lady who sang it.*

The opera season was followed by another event in September. A few kilometers away, the Payerne Air Base was the site of the greatest air show in Swiss history. It was called AIR14, and it was a celebration of 100 years of Swiss aviation. Four hundred thousand spectators attended the colossal event. The air space over my roof was a beehive of activity. I remembered the first time I had seen an airplane. It was over a hundred years ago, and I thought it was a bird. The B&B was packed for AIR14. An astonishing variety of aircraft from the last 100 years, including fighters, bombers, helicopters, and experimental aircraft, even a Jetman, could be seen everywhere in the sky. Phyllie's husband and his brother set chairs down in a nearby tobacco field to watch the event. The afternoon ended on a magical note as Bertrand Piccard's Solar Impulse floated silently over my roof like a huge dragonfly and faded into the distance.

The Payerne Air Base, which seemed to be establishing itself as a venue for mega-events, hosted the 44th edition of the Schwingfest, a Swiss Wrestling and Alpine Festival, called Lutte in our area, in 2016. A temporary arena was constructed at the airbase for more than 280,000 spectators. My rooms overflowed and camping cars filled my garden. A temporary stadium held over 50,000 spectators. People without tickets could watch the wrestling matches on giant screens, and anyone could watch the boulder-throwing and Hornussen competitions. Participants chose their prizes in a special pavilion. Crowned with a laurel wreath, the winner was sent home with the traditional first prize: a live bull.

Although the sport is particularly popular in the Swiss German area, we also had a club in our town actively supported by our mayor, who had been instrumental in bringing the national festival to our area. I heard all about the event when Phyllie and her friends returned home, enthusiastic but seriously wilted. The 32-degree temperature that week was amplified by the vast tarmac surface of the military airport. Installations of overhead mist, where spectators could cool off, became favorite meeting points.

With all these gigantic events occurring in our district, there had been no time for sunset chats with Phyllie, and I was pleased to find her sitting in her chair by the fireplace.

"You've noticed that we 're not a Bed and Breakfast anymore," she said.

Of course, I had noticed.

"Times have changed. New B&B's have private bathrooms, and guests are starting to expect that. The work is getting to be too much for me. We'll be doing only groups from now on. It will be easier for everyone. Some of our B&B guests will come back for their special occasions, so you will see them again."

I had enjoyed my B&B years. There was never a dull moment. I thought about all my favorite guests and was saddened that I wouldn't be seeing them next year. The most memorable were the ones the staff called the oldies. They were two sisters in their 90's from South Africa who came in a Dormobile; an ancient Vauxhall fitted out as a camping car named Bondo.

Each year, they left South Africa on a freighter for London.

There they visited friends, painting exhibitions and theaters, left on a ferry, crossed France, picked up their camping car stored in a garage in nearby Vallon, and arrived in Sisikon on the shore of Urnersee in the State of Uri to spend the summer. When the weather turned chilly, they left their campsite and arrived in my parking lot. The peak of the B&B season was over, fortunately, because they were both nearly deaf and shouted at each other at the top of their lungs. The youngest, a mere 91 years old, was an accomplished artist, and some of her watercolors found a place on my walls.

The oldies were nearly my age and, like me, had lots of stories to tell. They brought bottles of South African Chardonnay and told of their experiences as children during the Boer wars, subsequent rebellions, war of independence, apartheid, and sanctions. At the end of their stay, amid boisterous shouting and maneuvering, Bondo found its way out of the parking lot and onto the street. We all shut our eyes and prayed that they would arrive back at the garage in Vallon without causing an accident. There was some obscurity surrounding Bondo's insurance and license plates. Their departure left a blanket of silence and a sigh of relief, but we always looked forward to their arrival the next year.

Phyllie continued. "To help you to adjustment to your new life, I have made a new room for you and my husband in the annex," she said. "I'm putting a wide-screen TV in there for both of you."

I can't say how much I enjoyed watching the news on that big screen. The Swiss soap opera Lüthi und Blanc was back on the television as a rerun, and I could relive my glory days as a star.

There were lots of interesting programs, including one about our Swiss Guards at the Vatican. They received new helmets this year made with a 3D printer. The new helmets were made of PVC and had hidden air vents to keep the men cool in the hot Italian sun. They were created by a Swiss firm that scanned the 16th century original to produce a model and then painted it with UV-resistant paint. It took one day to make a PVC helmet, whereas the metal ones had taken a week.

I looked forward to hearing what guardsmen returning to our area thought of the new helmets.

The digital age had arrived. With 3D printing, 5G communication networks, and artificial intelligence, I suppose my calendar will soon be projected on my kitchen wall, and paper abolished forever. Even though I was well over a century old, I still attracted filmmakers. A young student director made a short film in my rooms. Suddenly, there was a strange buzzing gadget flying over my roof and around my façade. If I had arms, I would have swatted it. It hovered just outside my windows and photographed through the glass. The nerve...can you imagine? When I saw the finished film on Phyllie's computer, she explained a drone had filmed it.

"Cinematography has changed since you were a soap opera star. Drones can film from angles that were never possible years ago."

My observation of Avenue de la Gare was getting a little boring when the Buffet de la Gare, the oldest establishment in our neighborhood, started organizing classic car meetings on Friday evenings. From then on, fortunately for me, a parade of exciting cars passed in front of my gate every Friday. They were a mixture of vintage motorcars, hotrods, military jeeps from WWII, automobiles called old timers or new timers. Once a year, a reunion of vintage tractor owners assembled near the railway tracks and showed off their Hürlimanns, Cases, Ford-sons, and other early models. I was grateful to the Buffet de la Gare for putting on this entertaining show for me.

On November 11, 2018, there were commemorations of the signing of the armistice that ended World War I in every European country, including Switzerland. I vividly remember the signing of the armistice a hundred years ago and the joy of the population when that terrible war was finally over. I was young then and thought humans would evolve beyond settling their differences by killing each other. It's going to take longer than I thought.

Another commemoration was marked on my 2019 calendar.

It was a special edition for the bicentennial anniversary of Nova Friburgo. Two hundred years ago, our lakeshore witnessed the departure of a group of Swiss who left from Estavayer to found the colony of Nova Friburgo in Brazil. The commemoration on July 4th started with a Mass conducted by the Bishop at the collegiate church of St. Laurent. From there, the procession continued to the Place Nova Friburgo, where a sculpture marks the exodus.

In 1819, the Swiss, like much of Europe, suffered from poverty and hunger. A period of severe climate abnormalities due to volcanic eruptions and low temperatures culminated in an agricultural disaster and massive famine. The year 1816 was known as the *Year Without Summer*. Brazil, no longer a Portuguese colony, was moving towards independence. To promote a European-style civilization in the kingdom of Brazil, the King offered a colonization treaty to the State of Fribourg, giving its farmers travel expenses and free land in the mountains.

The dream of owning productive land, uninhibited by cold and frost, took root in the minds of Swiss farmers.

On July 4, 1819, after a solemn Mass in the collegiate church of St. Laurent, 830 Swiss departed from Estavayer to Basel to join emigrants from the Jura and other parts of German-speaking Switzerland. That year, 1088 Swiss embarked on a voyage of no return.

The first ordeal faced by the emigrants was a six-week wait in Holland for ships to arrive. There, they buried their first dead due to malaria. In September, they took to the sea. The journey turned to tragedy when storms broke the masts of the sailboats. More than 400 passengers perished. Prowling sharks devoured the dead. In December, the survivors finally landed in Rio de Janeiro and ate oranges and bananas for the first time. To the sound

of fifes and drums, the survivors marched into the mountains and inaugurated their new colony. The colony's first
local council was established, masses celebrated, and the
children met their schoolteacher, Bonaventure Bardy.

The Swiss colonists cleared and burned the rainforest
and turned it into cropland. When the soil proved to be
poor, the more determined emigrants turned the virgin
forest into pastureland that resembled Gruyère or the
Pays d'Enhaut. Others turned to the cultivation of coffee
with labor supplied by slaves. Nova Friburgo became a
supply center and axis for the transport of coffee en route
to the port of Rio de Janeiro. The colony continued to
prosper, but its ties to Switzerland were gradually lost.
Contact was reestablished in 1973 after the publication
of "Genèse de Nova Friburgo" by Martin Nicoulin, giving
birth to the Association of Nova Friburgo.

Phyllie sat in her chair next to the fireplace, and I
looked forward to our familiar chat.

"I have been notified that the town has approved a new
urban plan," she said. "Our residential neighborhood that
has become an industrial zone will become a residential
neighborhood again."

That was news I had waited a century for.

"You'll soon be 110 years old, and I thought a facelift
would be an appropriate birthday present."

It was very thoughtful of her, and I thoroughly enjoyed
my make-over. Two handsome young stone cutters renovated the columns holding up my portico and repaired my
windowsills.

They spent days sanding my stonework. It felt lovely,

like a soft massage. The faded woodwork under my roof was repainted. Reaching my roof is not an easy matter. A truck with an elevator platform attached was brought into my garden. The painter moved the platform up and down my façade. I quickly got used to having him bobbing around me and missed him when the work was finished. The paint on the masonry of my façade, put there by Phyllie herself in the 1980s, had remained in perfect condition. Three of my second-floor storm windows that had been missing for 50 years were replaced, and a modern heating system was installed. Some attention was given to my basement. I cannot stress enough the importance of a dry, healthy basement. When spring came, a fountain appeared in my water basin. It shot up at 10:00 in the morning and disappeared at precisely 18:00. It was very punctual.

I was now in good shape and ready to face the next century.

My neighborhood, on the other hand, had not improved.

Square, roofless modern buildings were appearing everywhere. Regrettably, I could no longer see the rooftops of the town or the Sacred Heart Institute.

The sisters who had run the institute for a hundred years were too few and too old to manage it anymore. They sold it to the town to keep it running as a school. After modifying the building to meet modern standards, the community possessed a magnificent school building and grounds for future generations of children.

Knowing the hundred-year cycle of human events as

well as I do, I should have seen the epidemic of 2020 coming.

It started out bad and got steadily worse. News reached us that a virus called COVID-19 had appeared in China. With lightning speed, it invaded Northern Italy. Our Swiss-Italian border was the first to be affected and then the rest of the country, Europe, and all the world. Stringent restrictions were placed on the population. The elderly were confined to their homes.

Younger members of the family and volunteers did grocery shopping for them. School children and office personnel worked on computer screens. On the positive side, the virus brought my environment back to what it was when I was young. There were no airplanes overhead. The sky was blue without traces of condensation trails. Fewer cars passed my gate on Avenue de la Gare, and pedestrians wore masks. The birds were singing louder, or I could hear them better. No one knew how long the virus would remain among us or what our future held.

Phyllie stayed at her husband's house in the country during the pandemic and came by periodically to see me and take care of my garden. Our borders were closed, except for foreign workers. Schools and non-essential businesses were also closed. The daily news kept us informed of the steadily rising number of cases and deaths. It was exactly what I had experienced in 1918 with the Spanish Flu. Tents were again constructed outside hospitals, but instead of care being given by the Catholic sisters, this time, the army backed up the exhausted medical personnel.

Again, our newspapers were full of funeral announcements, and mortuaries ran out of space to store coffins awaiting burial.

Our Surrexit procession, after surviving for centuries, was canceled, as well as our antique fair, markets, and other public events. The noble brotherhoods in our town held virtual assemblies. My rooms were empty, cold, and silent. No more than five people were allowed to congregate indoors at a time. A month into the lockdown, my newspapers shut down due to a lack of advertising. Fortunately, the renter in my studio had her television on so I could stay informed.

By the end of May, the first wave of the epidemic had subsided, and the population returned to almost normal activities, albeit with face masks, disinfected hands, and social distancing. During this short interval, I enjoyed a wonderful event in my rooms and in my garden. It was the wedding of Jim, Phyllie and Jack's son, to Katja, a lovely German girl. It was the only good thing that happened to us that year. In November, a second wave blanketed the country and was even worse than the first. A third wave looked imminent in the spring of 2021, but the most vulnerable population had been vaccinated by then. I had noticed for some time that Phyllie was looking tired.

The epidemic had complicated the management of my space and placed a hardship on our personnel. Three months of reservations had to be canceled, and deposits returned. I was beginning to feel guilty for having burdened her with the writing of my memoirs. She often perceived how I felt, and I wondered if she had come to the same conclusion. In any case, my story was now up to date and couldn't go any further.

As the sun set over the Jura and the shadows lengthened in my living room, she sat in her favorite chair, waiting to talk to me. "I'm going to stop writing your memoir now," she said.

"I'm no longer young, and I want to devote my remaining time to other things. I know you have a long life ahead of you, but the next decades will have to be written by someone else.

I feel sure someone will step up to the task."

It was a shock, even if I had expected it. The human life span is too short for me to keep the same owner throughout my existence.

At least, my future owners will have my written memoirs to guide them, which will make it easier for me to manage them.

What could I say to the two widows, Madame who built me and Phyllie who restored me, after all the years we had spent together, except...

Thanks for the memories and for taking such good care of me!

The Villa St. Pierre

Bibliography

*The official historical document of The Villa St. Pierre and
its geographic occupation during the Middle Ages by:
Daniel de Raemy, Service des biens culturels SBC,
Monuments d'art et d'histoire du canton de Fribourg
Le temps de la Mob en Suisse romande, 1939/1945
La Suisse dans les tempêtes du XXe siècle
The New York Herald European Edition, August 4, 1914
Swiss will fight for Neutrality
The New York Herald European Edition, March 14, 1916
Nearly 2,500 Huns want to be Swiss.
The New York Herald European Edition, June 5, 1916
Italian Hour advanced – French daylight saving scheme
The New York Herald European Edition, November 12,
1918 - Text of the Armistice conditions
Etude historique de la littérature fribourgeoise, Imprimerie
St-Paul 1907 ; Bernard de Vevey
Louis Grangier les Nouvelles Etrennes fribourgeoises 1942
La Liberté du 6 janvier 1892 et du 23 novembre 1964.
Annales fribourgeoises 1925, 1926, 1928, 1929; 1932
Les Annales d'Estavayer de Dom Philippe Grangier 1905.
La Suisse et la Grand Guerre by George Wagnière,1938
Guides de Monuments Suisse, Estavayer-le-Lac, La Société
d'Histoire de l'Art en Suisse
Les Dominicaines d'Estavayer-le-Lac, 1316 – 2016
Switzerland from earliest times to the Roman conquest
Les niveaux des Lacs du Jura, Hanni Schwab & R.Müller
and numerous other works.*

About The Author

The author was born Phyllis Ellison in Northern Wisconsin in the United States. She came to Switzerland with her American husband on her honeymoon and never left. Her first book, published in 2017, is the mystery *Rendez-vous at My Lady's Manor,* set in the Villa St. Pierre during her Bed & Breakfast period. For more information, visit www.myladysmanor.org.